Zero Point Living

Transcending the Matrix through Universal Law

Faith Nouri

TABLE OF CONTENTS

Illustrating the concept with Questions and Answers

1. Conversation with Mary;
2. Conversation with Sima;
3. Conversation with Jamal;
4. Conversation with George from Mexico with Faith;
5. Conversation with Sherry;
6. Conversation with Alex.

ISBN 978-0-99971880-0-3(pbk.)
ISBN 978-09997188-1-0 (e-bk)
Cover Image: Grandmother Spider - The Weaver ©
Jo Jayson
Back Photo by Angela Chow
Library of Congress Control Number: 1-
6067305581

DEDICATION

To my loving daughter Natalia, and my soul sisters and brothers, with my love and affection.

ACKNOWLEDGMENTS

I thank my wonderful daughter for her unconditional love and support.

I thank my soul sisters and brothers. I acknowledge my dear friends Sally, Kerry, and Maria for their friendship, unwavering authenticity, support and love in assisting me in creating a space to make this book happen.

To my dear father who crossed-over in 2009 - I am so grateful for having you in my life and sharing memories and experiences together.

To my family for gifting me with all the possibilities and experiences in this virtual reality.

My heartfelt thanks to all who touched me in my journey. I realize that every incident and experience was meant to bring me to this point of where I am.

I thank Andrew Rodriguez and Terry Huttayananont for your heart-felt support and your assistance with the interior and exterior presentation of this book.

I am grateful to Kelly G. and Rodrigo C., two fantastic shamans.

I thank many authors who took the role of being my teacher, starting with Dr. Wayne Dryer. I can think of about 50 courageous souls who candidly shared their knowledge and experience with me. Your wisdom touched me in so many ways during my continuous growth. I thank all the devoted coaches and teachers of various workshops who inspired and guided me when I needed your insight and expertise.

To the volunteers who shared their experience candidly and assisted to bring the concept of this book to life, I thank you for having faith in the potential of this project and thank you for participating.

I am grateful beyond words.

About FAITH

Fatemeh Faith Nouri was born in Tehran, Iran in 1966. After graduating from high school and the turn the country took shortly after the Islamic Revolution, she came to California to study. She graduated from California State University, Northridge with a major in Political Science in 1992. Due to the economic downturn that affected her family, she decided not to pursue law school after college and instead moved back to Tehran to learn from her father who was running a successful import/export business and enter into international trade. Ms. Nouri soon found success working as an executive for multi-national companies, as well as a project manager of a major Iranian Government contractor that built the first ever shopping market chain in the country. At the grand opening of the chain, members of Congress attended the event, but Ms. Nouri was politely asked not to attend the grand opening of her own project because she is female. She received no recognition for her work on this major project because of her gender. This experience among others led her to leave Iran in 1996 and relocate to Canada. In Canada, she decided to pursue a career in law; she graduated from law school and worked in Vancouver, British Columbia for one year. In November of 2000, she moved to California to be close to her immediate relatives. Ms. Nouri passed the California Bar in June of 2001 and began working as a lawyer in Southern California at that time.

Ms. Nouri is a dual licensed attorney, handling U.S. and Canadian matters. She became a Certified Family Law Specialist, a designation granted by the

State Bar, and she is a collaborative divorce attorney, minor's counsel, and mediator. Ms. Nouri's practice includes cross-border, immigration and international matters.

In the Summer of 2013, Ms. Nouri took a mindfulness class at the University of California, Irvine and attended their retreat at Joshua Tree. Here she was exposed to writings by Ding Le Mei at the Institute of Mentalphysics. This encounter sparked a thirst for knowledge that propelled Ms. Nouri to study works by Jane Roberts, Louise Hay, Wayne Dyer, Eckhart Tolle, Tom Campbell, William Buhlman, James Twyman, Charles Leadbeater, Gary Zukav, Annie Besant, Helena Blavatsky, Dolores Cannon, Robert Monroe, several modalities of healing books including Pranic Healing, Dr. Bradley Nelson, Teal Swan, Andrew Bartzis, Lee Carroll, Uell Andersen, Eben Alexander, Anita Moorjani, David Hawkins, Dr. Brian Weiss, Joseph Benner, and many others.

In 2014 Ms. Nouri was able to connect with her higher self and understand what it means to be in the "void" or "abyss" as some would call it. She was able to heal her physical body and began working on healing her emotional body. During her personal healing and soul-searching journey from 2014 to 2016, she had several experiences where she connected to her higher self and found guidance. In October 2017, she had a complete shift during her journey when she faced her fears, doubts, barriers and belief system, that obstructed her ability to connect with and experience total fulfillment and those obstacles lifted. She experienced living with unconditional love in this matrix. Zero Point Living is her first book sharing what she experienced and offers a guide for others to shed their belief system, fears, and doubts and to live a fulfilled life. This book is meant to create a shift in the reader, starting with self-awareness and then healing if the reader is ready. The intent is to answer pressing questions such as "Where I am going?", and "What is my purpose?"

Ms. Nouri suggests readers also read *The Power of Now* by Eckhart Tolle and utilize Byron Katie's *The Work*, in conjunction with the guidance offered by this book. This book does not undertake to repeat the work of these two excellent authors.

INTRODUCTION

It started on <u>Friday morning</u> of October 20th between sleep and wake, with my eyes closed. I saw so many geometric shapes and a large spider on my third eye (ajna chakra) with a small spider by its side. I woke up, and when I closed my eyes I did not see it again. I asked a few friends what it meant to see a spider. Two friends wrote that a grandmother spider appears to teach wisdom, and that I should be ready to learn something new. I dismissed it.

On Friday evening, I met the shaman that I had heard so much about. She spoke about identity and putting masks on our faces. I was not listening much, as I gathered that I have more knowledge in this area and felt our beautiful Shaman was not well read. I thought I knew better. After all, I am an educated and respected attorney.

That <u>Friday night</u>, I set my intent: having a mystic experience. I had one in my journey. I saw a spider web. The spider showed me myself. Then I heard myself telling me, "Look at yourself." What I saw was myself with webs and strings attached to every part of my body. All of the strings were attached to me and each string or web was a belief, perception, and built barrier. It was me showing myself how I have warped myself with my cultural and social rules and how it was causing me to live my life.

On Sunday, I set an intent to let go of judgment and access my knowledge. That morning, in the wee hours of early morning, I looked within myself, with the spider helping me to see. I saw myself again with strings attached to every part of my body. I was attached to webs. I asked myself "Why?" I saw a picture of myself not being honest with myself. I could not understand the connection. I kept asking "Why string?" I saw more pictures of me hiding from myself in conformity. I was shown another picture of event showing me accepting things, even when they were going against my inner self. I saw pictures of past events, where I acted as I thought I should act based on expectations, conformity, perceptions, and belief system, I also saw myself acting out of fear by not being who I am. I was vulnerable and scared to discover that I was not what I projected myself to be. The farce was a facade created by me. I created the webs and then connected them to myself. I confined myself with the webs, yet I could not understand why I felt so suffocated. I did not understand why I was not me because I did not know to be anything else. I assumed what I was, it was indeed me. But it was not. Once I saw the facade, the layers, I realized. I then saw the faces of my fears.

I asked, "Where is it coming from?" I was shown pictures of my acting out of fear: fear of inadequacy, fear of discovery, and shame. I asked "Who sets these barriers? Why?" The answer was that barriers are there to protect me. I asked, "Protect me from whom?" I kept asking and I kept seeing pictures of me in different situations throughout my life. All of a sudden, it became apparent. The shock of it to realize, the one who has built layers and layers of barriers in the name of protecting me, is no one but me. Then came the question, "Why would I need protection from myself?" The moment I asked that question, I recognized the answer. The barrier crumbled. The walls that I built came down.

Part 1

HOW BARRIERS WORK

Through life we build barriers to protect ourselves from danger. Danger could be anything we perceive that we believe does not benefit us in reaching our goals, our agenda, or our daily life. Danger could be stopping ourselves from listening to a documentary and tell ourselves to change the channel so we won't learn or hear something our soul will enjoy. Danger could be when someone is showing us the road and we doubt the direction. Danger could be when we listen to our intuition, we doubt the message to let go of fear or shame.

The doubt and fear are our barriers. We are thought to trust our own barriers since the barriers are for our own protection. Barriers are our guards to prevent us from hurting ourselves. This is when we stop doing what we love because we doubt whether we succeed. We doubt because we trust the barrier more than our own abilities. We trust the barriers and by trusting the barriers, we fail to connect with ourselves. We built the barriers to protect us. But barriers are not for our protection. All are built in disguise. The thing that protects us is meant to sabotage us. We sabotage ourselves with our doubts and barriers. Our doubts and barriers are our sabotage.

I felt that the realization freed me from doubt, fear, and I saw how "judgment" has been a big part of it all. Doubt based on judgments. We call it "judgment call." We call it "sound thinking." It is all disguised programming. We programmed ourselves so beautifully because we are very intelligent and powerful beings.

I felt a large grey cloud that was sitting on my shoulder is lifted. I never knew or felt it before. I had no idea that I had that burden. The weight was gone. The wall crumbled. I could breathe again as I have never before. I could hear and feel as I've never before. My heart was full of love and pleasant inner joy filled me. I felt fear dissolving within me. I realized what I am here for; I sensed my purpose. I felt how happy I am to be honored to be here and so grateful that I am to be me, how I love myself and everything in my life, and how everything in my life has been set to arrive at this stage.

My inner being was gently bringing realization, the knowing of what it means to be free of all the webs. How does it feel not to have strings attached? Breaking free sets you free. It feels like a beautiful breeze in a hot day. It lifts your soul and you feel alive again.

I remembered why I am here. I am here to bring awareness. So many soul brothers and sisters planned and worked tirelessly to set this up. I had come with assistance of my soul family to bring a message. The message is meant to bring a change. I am activating you and your DNA and announce that we no longer wish to compete. We must no longer compete. By ending competition, we will end hurting ourselves at the soul level. Let me start from the beginning.

We are a powerful being. Each of us is a powerful being. We, this powerful being, created our universe.

We are the creator of our world. We created this beauty. We are intelligent and the evidence of our intelligence is our creation. Indeed, you created it all. You, we, us - we planned it all. At one point, the virtual reality game was just a game. The game was to be a part of our creation and face the challenge of returning to our origins, to be ONE. To make the game even more challenging, we created multiple barriers. The more challenging, the more fun. We loved to play. We are so clever and we made clever games. We played the game fully engaged. The challenge was and is to breakthrough our fear, and barriers in order to return to love. We never experienced unconditional love in this virtual reality. Even a parent's love for his child is conditional. We only learned of conditional love. Self-discovery is the return to the state of unconditional love and to understand this, we must begin the discovery with self-love. The one who releases himself or herself from the web, is the one who acknowledges and is aware to honor, love, and Be. Know that the web is your own creation. You created a prison by wrapping yourself with your belief system, doubts, fears, and you have been mastered throughout each life. Once you are able to face and see your true self and set yourself free, you are able to recognize that you are playing a game and you are merely a player. All life material possessions and desires are meaningless when you realize there is no true value attached to any of it, except what you and others collectively associate with that thing in this universe in this time and space. When you are you, you no longer harbor fear because you know who you are and will not entertain the games of mind.

Part 2

THE INTENTION OF THIS BOOK

What is intended that you get from this book? The intention is to help you answer the following questions:

Who am I?
Where I came from?
Where I am going and what I am doing here?
What is my purpose in this life?

These are questions that I will answer in context of the Universal Law that we souls have created and agreed to abide by.

Let me make it clear: There is no purpose to fulfill outside of you. In life, you are learning to return to your true self by recognizing who is THE YOU again. If you feel a calling to pursue a career and you see that as your purpose or Dharma, it is because you convinced yourself of that false belief and you are attempting to fulfill a gap or lack within you. However, in pursuing that Dharma or purpose, you learn to empower yourself and by empowering yourself, you can easier break the barriers that you created for yourself.

We are the creators and we made the game very challenging in this virtual reality because we can as such intelligent creators do so. We placed more barriers and comportments in the brain and in the way we think for more challenge. There was never an intent to harm each other. We really enjoyed the game until at some point competition entered into our realm. We never knew competition and never recognized competition. By introducing that element into our game, we began hurting ourselves unwittingly. In setting up the games, we did such a good job that we no longer were able to distinguish who we really were.

Our Conditioning starts from birth so it eventually becomes challenging to see inner You, hear You. You heard what you believe you need or want to hear.

You are taught how to hear, what to hear, and when to hear. What you do not hear through familiar channels, you mistrust. Yes, this is how things started becoming even more challenging for you. Once competition entered into this game, we (part of soul brothers and sisters) realized we need to bring awareness. However, Universal Law has the non-interference rule. Therefore, we could not interfere with this world, our game and our creation. The rules and games were created by us and we all agreed to them. Once we began hurting ourselves through our complex and clever creation, we failed to take notice for the longest time as we were enjoying the game too much to take notice. We loved the game and still many do. Many attempts were made to bring awareness to the whole creation, us. All prior efforts failed either because the massage was skewed or it failed due to the subject not being able to break through the game.

A part of us decided to come in this time and space and to bring awareness. I am here to activate you with this truth. You are the sovereign being under the

Universal Law. You, the sovereign being have the choice to either change your way and make a change for better humanity and return to love, or to take the easy road. While the easy road is by no means easy, it is the most familiar road to you. The easy road will keep you in this familiar environment and you will continue in this virtual reality as you did before and you will continue not to acknowledge your truth.

What you know as your world is a virtual reality. A game created by us, you and I. As a sovereign being if you refuse to hear this message, you will continue playing in the game as you did before. You are hearing or reading this because that is the way it shall be. While we cannot interfere in the process, you know that you have a choice. If you choose to not accept this call, you will continue in this virtual reality and continue this game. At some point, you will realize and you will take notice and undoubtedly will join the rest of your soul brothers and sisters who choose to end this game in its competition format. We no longer wish to see the pain and hurt of our brothers and sisters. While you may think taking the easy road is easy, it is indeed the one that will continue to cut you from inside and scare your soul. Your soul brothers and sisters would like you to know that we need to return to our game in a non-competition format to avoid hurting each other. We recognize you are unable to see this from your standpoint. You are so engrossed in this game and continuously adding more complexity to the game making it even more challenging that you fail to recognize that this is no longer serving us, as one. We cannot be separate or be separate. We are not separate. We are One. We will wait for those who choose to continue the game until you are ready to join. We recognize that we are one. We are not going to hurt each other, nor will we act in any form and shape to do anything other than bringing awareness to once again remember.

This is a no separation, no competition universe. This is what we created together. For those who would like to remember and embrace the true you, read on. I am giving you the basic of our laws to remember. The laws are what We agreed to abide by and to respect and honor. It is not the Law as you know it in this virtual reality. It is not law for enforcement, nor for Conformity. It is the law governing where we came from and where we are going. It is a road map of our principal. On October 22, 2017, I merely remembered the law for sole purpose of sharing the same in an effort to remind you. I was an instrument, unbeknown to myself up until recently, here to deliver this message.

We are born here with no memory; hence the reason it took me more than half a century to remember. I had to remember what I remember now on my own by lifting the veil of barriers. There could be no interferences. All reading and souls who touched me were assisting me to learn to stand in my own power, embrace myself, and to heal myself.

By healing myself, I was able to see True self and touch my scars - scars that left me in pain physically and emotionally. Returning to each moment is like returning to your True self. I remembered who I am, what I am. I am here to assist you to discover the same for yourself. I am you and You are me. We are one.

Part 3

BARRIERS TO BEING

Let me define a few terms here for better understanding as we progress.

Intent: It is what you set to do. It is you, ordaining you to see or hear or be as you set out. When I intent, I activate my inner guidance to seek. My intent is me moving forward with knowing. When I say I intent to see, it means I set myself to see. It is me, and knowingly moving in the direction that I choose.

Love: State of being. State of now. State of absolute wholeness. I love because I am. Love is not a condition. Love is. It is ever present without any opposite. There is no opposite to Love. When you are not love, you are not present. State of love is the ever-present moment. Eckhart Tolle has already covered this topic of ever present or being in a present moment and I refer you to his book starting with the Power of Now.

Ask yourself, how do I see myself through my lenses?

We have forgotten to see ourselves and identify our true self. Self is not this body. Self is not existence, as existence never ceases to exist. Our identity is our creation. It is ever changing infinity of me being. When you identify you, you box yourself with limitations that you place on yourself with the identity that you now identify yourself. Identity is not you. It never was. My true identity is the state of being.

I am the ever present infinite being. I move in ever changing motion of life. I move with love and love takes me where I am. Light is me as is you. I am the ever changing moment as I choose to see.

I am here to tell you that you are not this limited body. You are not this limited knowledge. You are not this limited being as you see yourself through your lenses. You set the limited lenses and you are not able to see fully. The lenses can only see to the extent it is able to see within its existence.

There is no separation of body and soul. Body is a part of soul presenting itself in the image we choose. Body is what you perceive it to be at a given moment. The same body can be seen differently by me and you, as we set our different lenses with our limitations through our individual filters.

Filters are our layers. Layers are resistance. Resistance are layers within us wanting to protect, that is you resisting you. Layers are a part of us and it is so intertwined that it is hard to separate them from this being. Layers become a part of us and it guides us as we see fit. We set layers and layers can be deceiving.

Interconnectivity: I move within my energetic field that I have with understanding not to violate your energetic field. Yet, we forgot the power of our energetic field and do not understand its movement and its purpose anymore. We are blind to its movement as our senses cannot detect its field and its wave through what we call "normal" channel.

I am a being intertwined with you and all others. We move separately, but we are truly not separate. My love of life leads me to you who is me. With our blinders and our layers, we cannot see clearly. There is no separation. There is no ending, nor beginning. We are end and it's beginning. My vibration is my form of communication with you (me)

As I vibrate, I move.

We are beings with unlimited presence in every direction. I can be what I want to be. Life never dies. It is ever changing from inception. (Inception is an inadequate word to describe.)

I move with filters as it suits me in this virtual reality. We build the barriers to protect ourselves from our knowing. The barriers are our protective shield to keep us from interference by others, and of our sovereign identity. Our truth is cloaked to create acceptable perception as a tool to navigate in this world. The essence of it is our acknowledgment and to identify each filter with our awareness. By building barriers, I avoid facing my essence. Barriers are our own layers preventing us from seeing our truth.

Our truth is simple. It is to accept ourselves as we are and see ourselves complete and whole as we are. What we perceive to be incomplete is our own illusion within illusion. When my essence is seeking to show me my truth buried within layers, I resist it by creating doubt and fear. Disbelief is our number one self-sabotage. Doubt is self-sabotage. With so many doubts and disbelieves, we have no ability to see the road it is taking us. We meditate, pray, look within and when we see a flicker, we doubt as to what we see and what we touch within ourselves. Breaking through barriers become illusion, since the one preventing us to break through is no other culprit but our own self.

We negate ourselves by negating who we are. We adapt false self and false identity to hide behind and attempt to numb the need to know. Our truth is crying to be acknowledged. When we don't recognize our own need to be recognized, we build facade to numb the need.

Identity itself is a mask arising from the role you play. It is a role of accepting separation. It is a role to play in this weaved web of life as you know it. "Christ like love" is a concept that is misunderstood and never received. Your role leads you from day to day to feed your need to play in this role with all distractions you have created for yourself.

When you are born, you are shaped into your identity. We think we are, what is expected of us; we think we are what we want and need. We shape our daily efforts to fulfill the need or want.

By never acknowledging oneself, adapting others' perception, we shape our understanding of who we are through lenses of others, and then the "I" forget me. We enjoy emulating and playing God to feed our needs. The need is a false need as it is far from you, as you are not one needing self-approval, self-diagnosis, self-reprimand, and self-punishment. The you within you is free of all obligations and identity as you know it.

You come from love, since that is your start. You start from pure satisfaction of being you. You are whole. You do not move to meet anyone's expectations, need or want, including yourself. You have no need nor want.

This all started from a simple game within the game. We mastered multiple games and inserted layers after layers. Every time we were close to seeing, we made the game a degree more complex. Soon the game became so complex that we could not remember who created the game and its purpose.

Home is pure peace. You have no need as you know and understand it. You are never alone. You are never anything but being. State of being is the state of love as your existence is revered and celebrated by you. There is no competition as you know it. State of existence is your state of being and state of being is your state of love.

From the moment we are born, we are set up to build barriers, emotional traps, and lower existence feelings. In every created culture, you are thought in different ways the same things. The most common ones are that: you are inadequate, you are not enough, you are not complete, and you do not know. Within you, you know you are not genuine, since you recognize you within you, yet you have no ability to fully investigate, nor dare to see.

All these trapped emotions and unfulfilled needs and wants that you think you have runs you through your lives. Your parents tell you how to behave, how to think, what to do, and who you are. If you feel your inner guide and that goes against your belief system, your own barrier will work against you to tell you, you are wrong. You become what others say you are to fulfill the prophecy you hear. Even when you rebel, it is so against your teaching and your understanding that you self-sabotage rather than self-discovery.

Self-discovery is to see your doubt and fears as just doubt and fear. They all are barriers created by you to make your virtual reality experience even more challenging. We, the creator, created this beautiful and complex matrix of dualities with an intent to engage ourselves with it in perpetuity as you understand it.

Part 4

STRINGS

How do our actions affect us?

We move through life with strings attached. The strings are each our belief system, our cultural and social conformity that we accepted or adopted as our own. We move through life with these Strings that has placed us in a web of constraint. We do not understand our lack of ability to see, breathe, or hear because we cannot recognize what is holding us back.

What is holding you back is you with your perception and belief system that is attached to you. You move like a puppet with strings attached. You can't see beyond your next planned step. To get rid of attached strings and free yourself, you must acknowledge and recognize how you connected the strings on you and how it got attached to you in the first place.

Strings are rooted in our belief systems, cultural and social expectations, or environmental upbringing and religious background. You could release yourself from all the barriers with your knowing through self-discovery.

Once you acknowledge and recognize your attached strings, don't teach the same to your children and saddle your children with the same strings.
The within power is not in emulation, but emanation. This is how you start breaking the cycle. To accomplish that, we need a new format of schooling

where individuality and moving with motion as you feel is celebrated, not suffocated. This will require not to teach and seek adaptation, conformity for the child but to trust the child to trust herself and to hear his inner guide and follow it as he or she sees fit. There is no one correct method. Only your perception of what you think is the correct method based on your own teaching and emulation. There are limitless possibilities, if we could only have the courage to accept the child for who she/he is. There is no danger in doing that and to celebrate their individuality.

Know that Everything is planned by you in this universe with your intent. Your intent is a powerful part of you that you misunderstood or never fully understood. When you place your intent on another, you place your energetic field on the other person and enter their energetic field. You can impinge on their energetic field with your "need". Your need can be a burden to another as it enters their energetic field. This is how we affect others and they affect us. Acknowledge your need even if you think it is not pure.

Part 5

LAW OF ATTRACTION

Intent leads you through each day by each day. Your life is set through setting your intent. You normally set your intent based on expectations and belief systems adapted by you. Expectation can only fulfill what you think is to be true for you. If you feel you are inadequate, you move with fully owning that bellied belief, even when you try to project otherwise, you are unable to untangle yourself. This is how the law of attraction works. The true meaning of the law of attraction is to know that you only attract your belief. If you seek money, it is because you feel inadequate as a being. Feeling is fed by your belief system. You believe money will resolve the lacks within you and your life as you lead. By knowing that you have lack at your core belief system, you cannot attract. The only moment you can attract is when you resolve your core belief of lack. But once you do, you no longer need or want the money because you already know you are complete and money does not resolve anything. Money is merely a commodity for exchange in this physical world. You never needed any commodity for exchange. You created it to rely and depend on as an external element outside of yourself for distraction in this virtual reality. Money has no value except what you and our collective consciousness associate to it to be.

To BE is a state of existence. Once you recognize your perception and belief system is concocting thoughts by your mind to occupy you with distraction, you no longer perceive its existence the same. Knowing the illusionary aspect of this virtual reality, you can free yourself of its strings attached with its holdings through your belief system.

It is true that you attract what you know to be true. Your knowing as to who you are and not accepting the illusionary aspect, you can break away the charged energy of lack, incompleteness, and inadequacy lodged within you that was placed through generations after generations of not knowing. Once you release, you return to a neutral state or zero field state at which point there is no polarity within you. Since you feel no need and no longer feel the fear of lack, you are in a state of Being. You, in turn, attract abundance. The term abundance is misunderstood. Abundance is not synonymous to attracting money. Abundance is the state of being of not needing or wanting anything as you feel fulfilled within. You attract simply because you are not moving in this virtual reality with any charged energy of lack coupled with belief system that no longer serves you and it only meant to keep you away from embracing your True essence. You will have abundance and the material things comes your way as you move through life, since it gets attracted to you. You attract because you are. Being is a state of love and that is forever freedom and abundance.

Part 6

INTERCONNECTIVITY

We are all interconnected. When you move through life you influence others as others influence you.

How does interconnectivity work? Each person has his/her own magnetic field. When I am thinking about someone, I am sending energy that moves and connects to the other person's energetic field. If the person is aware of himself, this is when the other person remembers you or thinks of you or sometimes you immediately hear from that individual. You energetically call the other person, per se, to oversimplify the concept for picturing the concept better.

If you feel negative towards another, you equally send negative energy to the other person and that is the reason conflicts in relationships feed itself. You feed the conflict with your internal negative feelings and belief system. The other person feels the burden and your negative charge as it enters into their energetic field. That is the reason conflicts and charged energy remains within and between us for so long. Once a charged negative energy feeds within you for so long, it irregulates your system. By irregularity, your system, and your body malfunctions, per se (oversimplifying it for our purpose of explaining it here). Negative energies are energies of low grade that has a mixture of heaviness. If you are sensitive to the energy of others, you can distinguish a positive from negative energy. Negative energy is heavy and it has its own presence.

The presence is intrusive since it is unwanted, unwelcome, and contrary to your essence. This is where you could feel the charged energy through headaches or other ailments when projected at you. By removing yourself from that environment or situation, you can eliminate or reduce its presence in you and around you in your energetic field.

Consider every contact you have with another person as an invisible line coming and going through your body. Each feed from your energetic field based on your projection or others' projection towards you. You could eliminate the effect of negative energies toward you by keeping yourself in a neutral state without charged energy. Then you cannot be affected. You can only be affected if you are a willing participant and you hold mutual charged energy.

What is charged energy? Your feelings and emotions create positive or negative polls within your energetic field. If you have positive, you are light and others pick up on your energy as happy, peaceful, inspiring, etc. If you carry negative charge, you have heaviness within your energetic field and you tend to be irritable, anger quickly, and/or be consumed with your own thinking process as you feed the energy within you with your constant viewing or reviewing the same subject or inviting similar charged energy through thought process as they enter into the mix and your energetic field. When you move with or feed the negative energy, you find more conflict and you feel unsatisfied as the day unfolds because your energetic field picks up on the lower energies and reacts to it, or you attract the same to feed your need. Like attracts like.

Every thought has its own associated, charged energy based on its positivity or negativity until you are in the present moment. Once you are in the present moment, you are not occupied with thoughts and your field is no longer charged with thoughts running through your head. This is the reason "being in a present moment" is a state of being. Hence, state of being is the state of love, and acceptance. This is the state I call, "zero field," for lack of better term or word.

When you are moving through life with charged energy in this virtual reality, you paint your day with whatever charged energy you carry. You really have little power to create anything opposite from the current that is running within and around you when your thought process and belief system continues running in your head with all the possibilities and probabilities and past scenarios that create more of the same in your energetic field. Negativity brings more negativity.

If you feel sad, you have that feeling in your energetic field and as you go through your day, you attract more of the same or similar. Because our system is set up to sabotage us with hidden layers, we sometimes do not know why we feel the way we do. We start our day with confusion, impatience, and lack of desire to go on. Sometimes we do not even understand where it is coming from. Your program responds and activates this within you when you have these charged energies. The charged energy could have accumulated over time when you felt inadequate or unworthy among others and the feeling sits and brew as you would go through your daily routine. Doubt is the most common "culprit", for the lack of a better word. Doubt is your own creation planted in your system to make this virtual reality even more challenging for you. These are barriers that work against you but you feel it and think the barriers are there to protect you. We have fear of the unknown. Charged energy of Fear is nothing but layers of barriers created by ourselves to disguise it as protection layers when in fact it is a barrier against ourselves to see clearly.

Barriers are built over time since childhood. Every negative experience that had impact on you has left its imprint within you. The barriers are disguised and when you wish to breakthrough a habit or a belief system, it comes as your inner protective shield guiding you to continue the old habits and trends. It consoles you to continue the pattern. Barriers are roadblocks and are built by you to prevent you from a breakthrough from your thought process, perception, and belief system.

Consider the way you feel fear about a future event or a future possibility when you have so little information or knowledge of what the future holds for you. These barriers will keep you away from discovering yourself as it meant to do so. We created these barriers as a part of challenges in this virtual reality.

Once you recognize the barriers, you can lift the veil and break or dissolve them one by one. As you dissolve barriers, the veil gets thinner and you can see more clearly. This clarification is combined with feeling less restriction and you are able to make better choices in your daily life. You get involved in creating better choices within the realm of your desire. Your dependence to the same old habits becomes less and less as you create new ways to move forward.

Part 7

SELF-HEALING

Every difficulty or drama in your life has happened to progress you and by overcoming the event, you past a new milestone. Recognizing your efforts is very important. We could easily get caught up with our daily distractions to where our accomplishments are not noticed by us. We fail to stop, recognize, and congratulate ourselves for passing yet another milestone in our lives. By not recognizing and acknowledging, you do not give yourself and your body the opportunity to heal. The healing process is muffled. The solution is to review each event, see how you handled it, and then recognize your role and how you moved through it. Recognize that you today is the same you from your past. Acknowledge you and love you for your role as you played it in this virtual reality. Congratulate yourself and release the numbness that is left within you emotionally and mentally. The memory is there for you to recall and resolve. The emotion is there until you properly recognize it. Once you do, you feel the release and you no longer have any charged memory regarding that event. Thus, you empower yourself. This empowerment assists you to be more of you, who you are, which is a powerful being. This feeling of helplessness and inadequacy is the result of a lack of acknowledgment. Do not beat yourself up with your expectations by blinding yourself from what you really need to acknowledge. Acknowledge you, your role, and how you faced it. Your vision about what you call mistake or lack of foresight is not relevant. Disregard focusing on the challenge and learn to embrace yourself. Your act is not the same as your role. The act is a part of your learning process. Your role is to see yourself for who you are and embrace yourself once you do overcome the challenge. Overcoming challenge is not the measure of success -- it is you acknowledging yourself and moving lovingly to help and heal yourself. Feel your hurt and heal yourself. The challenges are so you can learn to love yourself and in the process of loving, you heal your wounds and scars. Wounds and scars are your badges of honor; learn to wear them with loving-proud, like a loving mother loving her child.

What is the purpose of life? There is no goal or purpose, but to Be. To Be and to love. The state of being and loving shall come when you break your barriers and face your fears and doubts by breaking your own barriers. (Barriers built from childhood based on your perception, adaptation culturally, religious, or the belief system that you lovingly cherished close to you as a part of your identity.) The real You is buried within all these layers and layers of barriers and You are waiting for you to see and acknowledge yourself. The true you is not judgmental; it is complete, whole and born to be loving. The real you loves unconditionally. Moving through challenges and acknowledging you makes you whole again as you were.

Part 8

NON-COMPETITION

You feed the despair within you with hope. God is you and you feel despair as long as you deny your authentic self. You do not need hope as hope is an illusion. Once you know who you are, you do not need hope. As a powerful being, you do not need to look upon an outside source for power created by you.

Know you are complete. Once you see others as a part of you and complete, you cannot see others as being less than you. Knowing that takes you closer to remembering who you are. We are one. I am you. There is no competition. Competition creates more dramas and distractions. Life is a distraction that we have created for ourselves.

There is no reason for competition, since your true self knows there is none, but that all competition are pure distraction -- it was created as a part of this game since inception.

Let's review the Universal Law in the context discussed.

Part 9

THE UNIVERSAL LAW

Universal Law is a guide as to how the Universe operates.

1.   _Non-Interference:_ We are a sovereign being in this Universe and we do not interfere with other sovereign. This means you are the one who will light your road and find your way back home. Home is you, within you. You come with no memory. Your lack of memory is a clean slate so you could have the opportunity each time to play your role and heal yourself. Healing can take place when you learn to see yourself whole again. To be is who you are. To be is to be love.

2.   _Law of Attraction:_ We do attract and create as we set out our intent. You can only attract what you are when you have no opposite within you. When you are unable to attract, it is because you have opposite polarity of what you desire in your energetic field and you are farther away from your desire. The more you press forward, the more you push your desire away from creation as long as the opposite polarity is activated within you and feeds from your energy.

Law of Attraction example: Let's say you want money. You have learned that you could visualize or affirm your desire to create. While it is true that thought becomes belief, it is inaccurate to think you can repeat a thought and lodge a belief system without polarity. That is oversimplifying a concept and it is contrary to the Universal Law. Your belief system becomes a part of you as you fail to recognize how quickly and smoothly it is operating in the background in a familiar environment (your familiar program). Your programming set-up is from habits, belief system, adaptation or perceptions, thought processes, and generated feelings. So when you ask for money, it is because you feel you do not have money or you don't have enough money to the extent that *you feel the lack*. That lack is rooted in your feeling inadequate, incomplete, not enough, undeserving or unworthy, or a number of other similar feelings lodged within you since childhood. Unless you eradicate or release the trapped emotions and replace these belief systems ingrained within your system, you cannot bring prosperity by visualization and affirmation alone. The lack has its own charged energy lodged within you; hence the polarity. Even though you focus and are in the present moment at times, it does not counteract your feelings of lack, if you have that within you. To be able to attract, you cannot have feelings or thought process or belief of "lack." But the feeling of lack is the reason in the first place for you to seek or desire more money.

You can attract when you are at zero point meaning you have no tug of war feelings within you and you have no lack within you. As such, you are not attracting the opposite since there is no opposite in You. You then attract what you desire as your field is clear BUT FOR the new desire and the energy naturally radiates. Again, the energy that radiates has no polarity. When you are at zero point, you already feel fulfilled!

3.   *There is no cause and effect as you understand it.* There is no Karma as you understand it. Let me explain. The cause and effect is how we navigate through life and the energetic field we bounce off each other. If you send a negative energy, you get that back. Know that you have no shortcomings, but what you label yourself to be. There are no bad acts from the past waiting for you to pay back in this life. However, if you believe in that, it is your doing and the effect is you sow what you reap. You set your action in motion with your intent and the belief system. If you lack any belief system, your intent is pure. Being the creator, you create what you intend.

If you hurt others, you are already hurting yourself. No punishment is necessary, since you do what you feel or perceive yourself to be. Nothing is outside of you. You hurt because you are already hurting. You lash out because you feel the lash upon yourself. No lashing out will set you free from your bounds and barriers until you face yourself and break away. There is no you against me. There is no you and me. There is only ONE. When you see someone is cheating another, he is not really cheating anyone but himself. There is an energetic connection that connects us; thus, the tug of war will continue within you until ending the war within. Release the negative energy and feel free again. There is no outside force doing anything against you that you already do not do it to yourself.

4.   *Non-competition:* There is no separation between you and I. We are one. Competition is seeking to be better than your soul brother and sister

in this virtual reality. But how could parts of the same shaping the whole be any different?

In the process of competing we have hurt ourselves since we are interconnected. What I do affects me and you due to our connectivity and our interaction. To see one better than another means to separate yourself and accept that a part of you is not good enough.

Know that separation is impossible. Once I see me against you, I have set my intention to separate and that intention does not sit well with "I" since there is no separation. By building stories and barriers, we numb ourselves. To numb yourself, you build multiple barriers and accept your own stories, so you can no longer see the unseen. <u>Victimization </u>is a product of your own thinking process of and about you. You can no longer feel your true feeling. The competition becomes a part of you in an attempt by you to fill a gap that was never in existence in the first place BUT FOR you own creation. The gap is "I am not good enough." The gap is "I am not one." The gap cannot heal until you recognize the fallacy in the premises. The fallacy is in opposition to your personal freedom as you know it. Personal freedom is a term that does not describe real freedom.

Real freedom is a state of being with no expectation and retribution. Real freedom is a state of being. It is a state of Being with no fear, no doubt, and no emotions that could pop up from time to time to tease you into actions. Real freedom is a state of moving through this virtual reality with knowing. In real freedom no person, feeling, and thought can interfere with your state of wholeness. You do not see yourself alone in this world because you are not. You do not have the need or want to be or have. You do not want or desire an instrument of chance, fortune, or luck.

IN CONCLUSION

We live in a virtual reality of our own creation. We are intelligent beings who created the Universe as we know it. We can only arrive at our point of being by not participating in the competition and mark our presence as a sovereign being with an intent to Be, the loving being who creates as she or he weaves the web of creation each day with her intention to love.

I attempted to illustrate the concept with your daily life questions, thought process, perception and belief system. The intent is to give you tools to see more clearly.

QUESTIONS AND ANSWERS

Conversation with Mary

Mary has two children and resides in Los Angeles, CA. She overseas research by big Pharma over the years. Mary is a healer and quantum hypnotist.

Faith: Mary, we had several conversations together. I'd like to break those down.

Mary: Yes.

F: I'd like to start with the intent. What would be your question about intent?

M: The purpose of intent, and the importance of intent.

F: What do you think is the purpose of intent?

M: Well I believe that there's endless possibilities in what we can create, and it is up to us to choose. Intention is very important to me, because it directs my focus and sends a clear message to the universe about what it is that I want to create. It is important to have clear intention so that the universe, the energy, can conspire with me, can help me to achieve that, to create that which I want. Intent gives focus.

F: Intent its guided through the way we move. Everything that is happening has the force of intent behind it. That energetic field moves it along. When we are setting our mind to do something, we think that it's happening on its own accord because we do not recognize that we had a role in that event to take

42

place. We mistakenly at times think that the intent is when we are aware consciously at that moment, in that specific time, and making conscious efforts for an event to take place but it's quite larger than that. A lot of times, intent is already within the way we are doing things, but it's so ingrained as a part of us, based on how our belief system is already set and the way we perceive things, that it's hidden and the intent is behind that, we just don't see it and feel it. As we move along our intent is there. The intent is what put the energetic field behind the current. For example, when you get up in the morning, you already had that intent to do what you're doing, you don't notice that, but it's already in motion.

M: Then what do you think is driving the subconscious intent?

F: We are the creator of it. We, with our thoughts, put the subconscious into action. And we send that energy out there, and we get the same energy back. The interconnectivity works in such a way that as I begin to move along in the direction that I am moving, either by absolute design or out of habit, which is again under my own design, or is programming, it's so intertwined that it's one, and we do not feel that, yet that in itself sends the force of it - for the lack of better word - out there and it's like a wave that expands. If my intent is to call and I pick up the phone and dial, it doesn't happen when you think you want to call and dial. It is already there, the action is part of the thought process that was already in motion, but it's very subtle. Intent is not just based on the focus that we put on what we are doing, it is part of our movement, and the way we are. It is ingrained in such a way that we don't even feel it.

We also are affected by other individual's intent and what they project onto us, and that projection reflects on the way we behave, and the way we take on their intent, and accept it and project it back, that's the interconnectivity of it all.

F: Mary, when you are struggling to do something due to fear or doubt, where do you think that fear or doubt comes from? Let's say you want to change your career to something more fulfilling, but you don't think that career change will be able to support your family. In that scenario, what is stopping you from pursuing that career change?

M: Well I feel that there are definitely layers of fear and doubt, and that I also feel that there are choices being made, conscious choices being made, even with the awareness of those layers of doubt and fear. I have chosen to define freedom within my current situation and in my current job. This is a choice that I'm making, but I am doing this because I don't want to experience a rebuilding, of having to come up with resources and a flow of money. I have decided that I don't have to choose one or the other; I've also taken into consideration the fact that I worked really hard at putting myself in this situation where I have a lot of freedom in my 9 to 5 job, so it isn't a clear-cut answer for me. I'm aware of the layers of fear, I am working with them, I suppose that this is a choice I've made to the next transition.

F: Accepting or telling yourself that you have freedom makes you comfortable, in a sense to take the burden you may feel, per se, of not fully doing what you want, and that justification feels comfortable for you.

M: It's more than that because right now at this very moment, I do not have all of the pieces together for me to be ready to start up a big project. At this very moment, there are pieces that are falling into place. At this very moment I'm not seeing the decisions to be made. If a decision needed to be made because the pieces were falling into place at this moment, then the decision could be made.

F: When you say pieces are not there, what do you think the pieces are, and where are the pieces?

M: I believe that some of those pieces are in the works. Just like everything before we woke up was finely orchestrated, that is still the case with the timing of the pieces falling into place. And so, the only difference now is that there's no need to feel that there is struggle, or that it has to be hard. Now it's just waiting for the pieces to fall into place, and to recognize the opportunities and then take action on them. The freedom comes in not being in a state of anxiety, anticipation, concern, or worry because you know that it's coming. You know that it is already here, and it is falling into place. That's where the freedom comes from.

F: When you are looking at moving along with your inner desire and you're waiting for the opportunity, do you wait for the sign you need for you to feel comfortable to move along?

M: I have to say comfort is not the right word. It feels is like excitement. It feels like "Yes this is it!" I have felt it before, and I recognized that it was my higher wisdom giving me the green light. It feels almost like obsession because the focus is so clear, so all it requires from me is complete action.

F: Regarding the layers that you observe. explain based on your experience and perception, how does the layer play a role in it. What do you see?

M: Usually in order for me to act on it with no concern, without hesitation, it has to be very strong. Other times there are messages that are strong but not as a strong, and the layers come in, where there's doubt, hesitation, fear and so there's a delay in my taking action, until the message becomes stronger. That's how I see the layers play out in these situations. For example, the land that I bought for the retreat center, I bought it in one week. I didn't even have the money, but I got focused and like, I was obsessed, but like, happy obsessed, a joyful obsession and within one or two days of looking, I found the property and then I bought it, and I had no questions or concerns.

F: Let's talk about how we can use our intent to connect with other people, to read other people's energetic field or to also connect with the spirit world. A while ago, I closed my eyes and I connected to a third person and his energetic field; I was able to feel what he was feeling. We both think that anyone can do that. Anyone can access that, and the reason behind it is that once we know what a powerful being we are, and we acknowledge that [power] within us, then the next step is to recognize that we can use this intent in a positive way. When we were entering another's energetic field, we were not intruding. We were not trying to attack anyone. We were making it clear at the beginning that my energy field is going to stay intact and with permission from higher self [and] from the third party, we're just entering to obtain information if the other person's higher self is willing to share. The difference between that and psychic attack is very different. Psychic attack is an energetic field, in which an individual person with an intent interrupts the energetic wave or field that is within a person. We are surrounded by our energetic field and there are vibrations that are in the form of a wave, that can be interrupted. If the person interrupting has the power, and the way they have the power is when they know, they acknowledge themselves, they're aware of themselves, and they know how to use their intent. That's when they become a powerful being because they know who they are, they know what they can do. We all are [that powerful], it's just [that] many of us are not aware of it or we are not acknowledging [it] within ourselves, and even if we acknowledge [it], we don't think we can [use it], and that doubt or lack of ability to see ourselves for who we are, makes it not happen. When a person is within their own power they can actually send the intent. The encouragement is to use the intent in a good way, but at times it can be used in a negative way. That's where psychic attack comes in. A person can get a headache, and that individual does not know why he or she got such a huge headache. Yes, it could be from the stress, but another possibility is through psychic attack. What are your questions that you would like to ask?

M: Is it appropriate to heal someone without their permission? Without obtaining their verbal consent?

F: Sovereignty is very important. We all are sovereign beings and the answer, based on what I know, is no. As sovereign beings, we have the right to choose and make decisions as to how we like to proceed. For another sovereign being to interfere and think that he or she knows better, that is really a violation of our sovereign being. Because when another individual, another soul thinks that they know better, that they know how we're supposed to live, how we're supposed to be, that's a perception, and a perception is not necessarily correct. A lot of times, since we set our life, [and] we set our tests and experiences for ourselves, it is for us to figure it out when the time is right, and the time may not be right. We are not going by anyone else's timeline, but [by] our own timeline and that's when the realization comes. Let's say you are sick. That sickness, it is something that you have wanted in this life, even though it sounds very cruel saying that you wanted to have pain, but it's not because there is a purpose beyond it, the purpose is a learning process. One we learn that, we grow. To think that another individual believes they know better for us, and then they try and take our pain away without us knowing what it is meant for us to experience, that individual is encroaching on our sovereign being and it takes away our right.

M: It would be encroaching on someone else?

F: Yes, on someone's sovereign being. To do that, they will take away that person's right to be able to experience [pain], in the way that the person set it up for themselves to experience, and that's not right. That means that [the interfering] person, that individual, who's doing it without permission, thinks that he or she knows better, and is acting as God (or its proxy based on the individual's perception or belief system). I use the word person because that's the best way of explaining it, but really it's a soul. We all are interconnected, but we all have our own purpose, and the purpose is to learn, the purpose is to heal, the purpose is to be able to break the barrier, break away all the barriers, and the belief system and perceptions we set up [for ourselves]. Once we break away, that freedom we experience, that is what we are here to get because that's when you feel the love, you feel who you are, you feel the peace, there's no longer fear and doubt, that's you.

M: How can one state their intention in a way that is powerful, in a way that doesn't require you to say it over, and over again?

F: Let's separate intent from belief. Your intent is what moves you. Your intent is what sets the stage for what you bring to yourself. When you are moving with your intent, you clearly state it to yourself. Acknowledge and clearly state what you set for yourself. Let's say my intent is to heal myself. If I'm looking at healing myself through energetic healing, then I set my intent to do it. As you do, you focus on what you want to do - which is to heal yourself, [and] then you will use the power within to draw the energy within you, and then you can focus on the specific area that needs healing and then project that energy [into that area]. It could be a white light. It can be a rainbow, whatever you want it to be and you focus to heal, and then your intent will state that I intended to heal, rejuvenate, and repair this area of my body. When you say that and you repeatedly do that for a period of time, then your result will come, but if you doubt when you do it, then you're not going to get that result because your intent cannot make it happen

49

because your disbelief negates what you were doing. It is important to make sure your belief system is not contrary to what you intend. The same goes with anything else. For example, [let's take] money. If I want money and my intent is to generate money, then I put this intent out there to only attract money and to do things that attract money, but if I already lack belief within my core, then that it will completely negate my intent, no matter how much intent I put into it. That is where the Law of Attraction actually comes from. That's why it doesn't work for many people, and that's why it becomes so frustrating for many people because they think that by just visualizing and affirming, it's going to happen. Visualization and affirmation are not going to erode the beliefs that you already have within you. That belief is most likely from childhood, when you were growing up. The belief that there's something not complete within.

First get rid of and eradicate all those disbeliefs. Once we set those aside, and are able to overcome those barriers, overcome those feelings of lacking, then you remove the polarity within. Without barriers and polarity, when you think that you want to have money, your intent can fly because there's only one way that it can go. That's the beauty of it. When you don't have doubt and fear, and you have that peace of mind within you, you feel fulfilled. Then you do not need to ask for anything because you don't even want anything anymore. You don't even need to ask, for the fulfillment attracts everything around you, everything that is good because that's how fulfillment feels. It feels that you're complete and that completeness attracts everything around you. You don't really go on and visualize money because you don't need to. That is a feeling that we are completely incapable of verbalizing.

M: We were talking about this earlier with the other healers, and there seems to be this commonality between healers, where there is a constant imbalance of financial resources. There seems to be some sort of power that is in opposition, some belief system that can maybe be affecting the individual but it feels like, because I see this, it seems like a commonality but there might also be something between the collective, and my question is what is that and how do we break from it?

F: It is correct that the collective can influence this trend you're seeing, but let's focus on the individual soul. To do healing, for the right reason, and I say that because of the intent of each individual who's in the profession for their own personal experiences is different. It may appear to be the same, but they all have variations based on their own personal experiences. Once a person's individual sovereign soul decides to pursue healing for the purpose of healing, either through enjoyment of it or because they feel that's their calling, each of those units of consciousness represents their own individual sovereign being and that sovereign being has to go through her own fears and her own reason. They are not able to make the money they want, the success they want, because if they dig deep enough within themselves, then they'll be able to see the belief that's attracting their reality. Let's just make an example here. Would you share the same opinion that making money as a healer is hard?

M: Do I share that belief?

F: Yes.

M: I can't help but recognize that there's a trend that I don't understand because there's lots of people who function under various types of fears, who do not have a problem generating financial abundance, and healers, especially some of the healers that I'm familiar with, have done a lot of self-work with their fears.

F: Let's talk about you. Do you share this belief?

M: I speak of it because I see it. I can't identify it. I can see that there's a flow that's sufficient to sustain the desire, but it isn't...

F: Let's explore the word "identify" in this context. When you started as a healer what was your perception of the healing profession at the time that you started?

M: I really didn't think much about the financial aspect.

F: When you first started the business, what were your concerns?

M: The concerns that I had with the business were wanting to make sure that I could generate sufficient income to be able to sustain the business without it affecting my finances negatively.

F: So that concern remained because you knew that it could become a burden on your family?

M: Right.

F: Generating enough income for it to be self-sustaining and not burden your family was very important?

M: Yes.

F: If it would have been a burden what do you think would have happened? What was your thought process?

M: If it's a burden even still now, my thought process... I don't know because I can't...I would figure it out...

F: In order for us to be able to eradicate that, we have to be able to acknowledge it. The barrier that you're not acknowledging, for whatever reason you formed it, it's already there. What is it that you feel within you? I'm trying to make the practical function of your barrier clear. If it's a burden, how would that affect your life?

M: It would affect my ability to sustain my lifestyle, but not so much for myself but for my family. It's more so for my family and their comfort.

F: Your concern is that it would affect your family. They could get upset with you because it affects them too?

M: I don't really care about them getting upset. I don't want them to experience discomfort.

F: Why don't you want them to experience discomfort? Is it because you really care about how they feel?

M: No, it ends up being because of how that makes me feel about my ability to provide and my ability to do my part.

F: You don't want it because it affects you. It is your concern towards them and maybe toward you, but it's a projection of how they would feel, their projection of you, would affect you.

M: Like if they would judge me for it?

F: What do you feel?

M: I would care about how they could experience more stress because I love my family and I want to help.

F: Then you're concerned about them. You don't want to put a financial burden on your family and that burden is on your shoulder. You had that concern of hurting your loved ones. So that concern feeds in. They way collective thought works is that you adopt the perception of people that are in the profession, causing you to have difficulties within your perception. Your thought process, it gets you to adopt the collective thought process in this area with other thoughts and then it becomes even more powerful.

M: This is part of what we're sharing?

F: Part of what you shared because you accepted that thought process. You first had it as an individual.

When you looked at projecting, you adopted the collective thoughts so you become one in that sense. In that aspect, that's how collective thoughts work. First you need to get out of the fear within you, but you need to detach yourself from the collective thought. Detach yourself from that thought process. They're not yours. Another person's ability or their perception of how to run a business could be completely different from yours. Their experiences are not the same as yours. So, now that you detach from that collective and start rejecting that thought process, you then need to deal with your own barrier. Let's discuss, when you think your concern about money started?

M: When? I'd say teenage years, when I started to become aware of the burden, because my mom always talked about how she had to work. We have my stepdad, and she had to work so it was never brought in her face that he had to take care of us or support us. She always worked because she didn't want to feel like a burden herself, and she didn't to make her own responsibilities feel like someone else's burden either.

F: But your fear of money started before. When did you realize how important money was?

M: I guess 6 or 7, but the only memory I can think of was me going around asking for money. I would go to my grandmother's house and they would give me some money. Then I would wait for my godfather to come home because he lived next to my grandma. So, I would wait for him to get home so he could give me some money.

F: But you were doing it, because you thought you had to do?

M: I guess I don't know why I did it.

F: Do you feel the burden? Look at that 6, 7-year-old girl. She's trying so hard.

M: I feel the burden of contributing.

F: Yes, you had this burden of contributing because you wanted to add in and to make it better. At some point you started wanting to not burden anyone with your finances. What age do you think that was?

M: It may have started since 6 or 7. I don't understand why or maybe I do. That memory that I have, I was living with my grandma. My mom was here in the States, and I was living in Mexico for about a year. So, at some level I must have understood the burden. I wasn't very conscious of it, but I must have understood it at some point.

F: Were your grandparents rich?

M: They were okay. My grandparents were not rich and my grandma worked selling food. Like, she sold tamales and other Mexican food.

F: Do think you may have heard discussion about money?

M: I'm sure I did.

F: At some point, you felt that you may be a burden?

M: Right and actually even not so much the burden, but what I couldn't tolerate since I was little was if somebody needed something, it affected me a lot. Like when my mom was like "I can't find my keys" or something similar, it was intolerable for me. I had to go and look for it and resolve it.

F: You wanted to be useful. You wanted to be useful by helping them out, to alleviate their concern or pain, whatever it was. Even if it was just finding a key, it was important for you to be useful and be able to do something for what you received in exchange. That has been within you, and you've carried that through your life and into adulthood and into your marriage. That's why you are carrying the burden for the family.

M: Yeah, I do feel that.

F: And you like to do it because it puts you in control, but why do you need to control this?

M: Control pacifies my insecurities. If I can control it, then I can keep it. I don't have to worry about things going wrong.

F: The bottom doesn't fall out.

M: Yes.

F: When did you feel that you have no control over your life?

M: I was very young. My parents were separated and my mom was here, and I was in Mexico.

F: At what point did you feel that you were in control? Looking at your life, was there a point in your life that you thought "Now I'm in control I know what I'm doing"?

M: It didn't happen until high school.

F: Before that. Let's look at when you were a little kid. You were being very useful, even indispensable, and that for you was very important. It was giving you control. What age?

M: I want to say 8 or 9, something like that.

F: That's the age you learned that if you can keep control, then you won't have unpleasant surprises. Control has become a way for you to avoid unpleasant surprises, and that's why your fears are all part of control. You do not want to lose control. Money helps to preserve control. If you will lose control, it brings concern for the family, which reflects on you and you don't want that. Opening a business, having that thought within you, lodged your thought process, and negated your intent. Now that you know what causes it, you have an awareness and you are able to see the inadequacy and the lack that you perceive and now you realize it's not there. There's no reason for you to feel that, "You need to be useful in order for you to be able to have what you have", or "You need to have control in order to have what you have". You only have everything you have because of who you are, and those belief systems that you adopted can be disregarded. You are completely full, there's no inadequacy. The barrier that we build prevents us from seeing ourselves for who we are. That's what barriers are. Once you see the barriers, you realize that you don't need them. The reason you're not thriving is because your intent is conflicting with your inner belief system. Now that you know, you are able to remedy your belief system. Every time your thought process says something negative, tell yourself "that's not true", "I'm good enough", "I can do it", "nothing is going to happen and I'm just going to move forward because I know I'm able to do it". You're not doing it for anybody else. The part of you that wants to see you, not for the role of others, but the other part of you. You can have a successful business. You can have success beyond your imagination, but if you carry that fear and doubt, it the negates your intent. The same is true with every single person because our intent can only carry so much, and that inner feeling that we have, which we are not aware of in our subconscious, can take us the opposite direction.

I get that you have this image that you build for yourself and you're comfortable with it, and you want to protect that and be that but when you break the wall behind it, there is another person down there who wants to be free.

M: That's what I was doing right now while you were talking. I was tracing back and I was looking for that part of me. Two things: one, I traced that these are the same traits that I describe with my mom. She overextends herself and gives, and she likes to see that as a reflection of her value. I see there's a connection there, sort of, like, lineage. I want to say that's true for a lot of the women in the family, but on a personal level, there's a disconnect emotionally early on in childhood. Where that disconnect happened I don't know, but I feel like maybe when there was a disconnect, that's when I began to modify my behavior and adapt my belief systems as coping mechanisms and ways of being more in control. There's an aspect of me that I haven't been able to get to.

F: When your parents were going through a divorce, how did you feel when they sent you to Mexico? What did you think about yourself?

M: I know that there's feelings that I was not important enough, not having enough value to be able to make things right, to be able to deserve for things to be right.

F: What else?

M: Well there's the worthiness. Not being worthy of what others had, such as having their parents together, and having their parents put them first. I was very emotionally needy too, or not so much needy but I had a strong desire to connect deeply that I couldn't have.

F: Did you feel loved?

M: Not really.

F: That's where it started. You felt not loved. You felt that nobody wanted you. You felt discarded and hurt. You started being useful because you didn't want anyone to discard you again, and then you started figuring out how you can add value to yourself. Then you started having your persona. You are a very strong, powerful being, and you had this barrier - this wall - that you built, and you weren't seeing that. When you break it, which you are doing right now by acknowledging it, you merge into one and you need to do that, because the "you" is not completely "you". It's not your true "you", as your true "you", that little hurt girl with all her feelings, needs to come to and merge with "you" right now. When you do that, you can recognize and realize how her pain has played a role in your life. You can fill those gaps that you have right now. You weren't acknowledging them because it was too scary to acknowledge them, but that's how you put yourself together. You know who you are, but a part of you has buried herself. You need to unbury that part. You have to acknowledge all of those feelings and celebrate them for who you are, because you accomplished that. You never imagined as a kid, that you would be where you are right now.

M: Thank you.

Conversation with Sima

Sima was born in Iran and she came to the United States when she finished high school. Sima is now in her 40's and works as a scientist for a pharmaceutical company.

Sima: I have a hard time saying "No". It seems that I just can't do it.

Faith: Why do you have a hard time saying No?

S: I do not know. I never thought about it.

F: Can you recall, at one point in your life, when you started pleasing everyone? How old were you?

S: Maybe after marriage.

F: So were you able to say "No" prior to marriage?

S: No.

F: See yourself as a little girl. Did you want to please everyone?

S: I do not recall wanting to please everyone.

F: When do you think you had a hard time setting boundaries for others at your own expense by saying "yes," when you did not want to do that anymore?

S: (No response)

F: Do you think this is cultural? Did you have "rodarvaysti" as a Persian -- meaning to be ceremonial without expressing true feelings?

S: True, that is correct. I had rodarvaysti.

F: When do you think you felt you had to please and

could not express yourself because you may have been concerned with not hurting another person's feelings, or you did not think it was acceptable culturally?

S: Part of it is when you are brought up with that culture, you inherited that, and you think that is how you are supposed to behave.

F: Do you agree that you were taught through your culture or society to behave the way you did because it was the accepted or expected behavior?

S: Yes.

F: Is it fair to say that you consented and you became accommodating because that was the expectation?

S: I remember from childhood in our culture how we do not live for ourselves, but we live for other people and that is expected of you.

F: When do you think that started?

S: From childhood.

F: So, you started having a set belief system based on how others expect you to behave, what others think is proper behavior, is that right?

S: Correct, we did.

F: Let's say it is current time and you just returned home from work at 6:00 p.m. and you are making dinner for the kids while they are doing homework, and you plan on resting after a long day at work right after dinner. Let's say in our hypothesis that a relative calls you at 6:30 p.m. that evening and says, "I am coming over at 7:30 p.m. to have tea with you and chat."

What is your response to her? If you say "Yes, come over," what prevents you from saying, "I am tired and don't come tonight and let's do it another night"?

S: I feel if I say no, it is lack of respect. I think I may hurt the other person's feelings. I have so many Persian values, which are not necessarily good values and I think culturally it is rude to not be hospitable.

F: How do you feel when you welcome the other person to come to your home when you really do not want any guests at that time?

S: Frustrated at myself first because I did not say "No." I also feel exhausted because I have more work to do as a result by cleaning the house now before they arrive, due to our culture. So, I am saddled with more work before the guest arrives.

F: How do your children and spouse react when you inform them that someone is coming over? Do you deal with their emotions?

S: Yes, I have to deal with their emotions.

F: How does that make you feel?

S: It creates conflict within the family because my children and spouse may not want that.

F: Do you see how you ignore your own feelings?

S: Yes.

F: Do you think you are going against your own integrity of telling your own truth?

S: Yes.

F: Are you doing it because you feel it is expected of

you?

S: Yes, I am trying to respect others at the expense of disrespecting myself and my family.

F: Why do you think when someone is asking you to come to your home, it is disrespectful to that individual to say, "This is not a good time for me and let's do it another time"?

S: I think it is just the way we are raised culturally.

F: Do you think your denial of saying your truth has any connection to your view as to your self-worth?

S: I don't know.

F: Do you accommodate the other person because you think that is what a good person does?

S: Yes.

F: Do you see that your belief system is inconveniencing you?

S: Yes. You are right. Now I see and want to know what is in our culture that makes us do this.

F: That is just conditioning. You learned that.

S: True.

F: The longer you ignore your true feelings to please others, the more you no longer show your true feelings as a habit because you are too busy pleasing others.

S: True.

F: What do you think that does to your self-respect and self-worth?

S: Realistically, that is the case. For example, at work, if you are not efficient, you are out of work. If you do not do what is expected, you are not a good mother or spouse or child.

F: I am hearing you say, "If you do not do what is expected of you at work, then you are not good enough. If you do not do what is expected of you as a parent or spouse, then you are not good enough." Is that what you are saying?

S: Yes.

F: Your measure of your value is based on what you can do for others.

S: Yes.

F: When you are measuring yourself based on what you can do for others, you measure yourself through their eyes and how they perceive you and your actions. What do you think about this statement?

S: Yes, that is true.

F: Do you feel most people appreciate your efforts?

S: No.

F: Do you think that is because you do not appreciate yourself when you are in the process of pleasing others?

S: Yes, that could be it.

F: When you interact with others and do not say your truth, you do not listen to your heart. The reason you deny your truth is because you have the fear of being yourself or speaking your truth. Your fear is that if you start saying no, there may be consequences for you and you are not ready to face them.

S: Yes.

F: When you interact with others, you project your energy to others, which is based on your feelings and they are picked up. That projection could be helplessness or the need to please others. Until you tackle this belief system within you, and do not see yourself complete, you will continue to project the same. Feel good about yourself. See yourself for this beautiful and accomplished person that you are. Find out what you like. As long as you continue this game by not being yourself, you deny your truth.

S: How do I get to my true self?

F: Acknowledge to yourself that, "I am going against my own integrity by saying Yes when I really want to say No. I am doing the same with my family and everyone is comfortable with the way I behave because it suits their needs and it is not their fault." You need to recognize that you cannot own someone else's perception or belief system when it goes against you and your true feelings.

After acknowledging it, stop repeating the same trend. That will surprise many, but it is not about them. You cannot go through life not loving yourself, not being in touch with yourself, and not seeing yourself. As someone once said to me and it worked, "Go through your picture album and find pictures of your childhood with fake smiles." Remember that and heal yourself. Acknowledge that pain you went through. This is a map towards happiness. You have hidden yourself and your true feelings from yourself and others because you did not think the feelings were acceptable. You put other people's feelings paramount over yours. Start now. Acknowledge yourself. Every time you want to say something that goes against your true feelings, decline to take that path. You now have the awareness and now you can take a different path. Many will be surprised because they are used to throwing things at you, and having you take it.

What is holding you back is your fear of saying "No." Your fear, that if you say no you will lose their love or their friendship, is an illusion. Once you see yourself worthy and trust yourself to express your true self, you start the process of getting rid of strings that you attached to you, which were created by you. These strings are your belief systems or other people's perceptions that are adopted by you. You learned to behave in certain ways. You limited yourself to protect yourself. Once you place your fears and doubts aside, you can see fears and doubts are just illusions. As a child, you accepted a belief system or other people's perception of you as your own. This in turn limited you to only act in certain ways and you forgot who you are and what your true feelings are. You do not permit your true feelings to be expressed.

S: I blame my parents for it, but I know it is not their fault because they were brought up in the same culture. A lot of things we teach our kids are absolutely wrong. We always live for others in our culture. We do not live for ourselves based on our culture. If we do something and it is not pleasing to others, we are concerned about the consequences. The mind process keeps going on and on in the same track. In the end, we do not realize that we are hurting ourselves. We are not respecting ourselves.

I was taking classes to perfect my communication skills because I thought my difficulties of being overburdened with the workload from my co-worker and employer, and not being recognized for my work, was due to my communication skills, but it is not. The way I view myself spills into my work.

Conversation with Jamal

Jamal was born in the United Arab Emirate, and is of Muslim background. He came to the United States to study and has since stayed here with his wife who is a US Citizen.

Faith: I would like to know if you have any question you want to ask?

Jamal: Yeah, law of attraction.

F: Law of attraction with regard to money?

J: Sure, yeah.

F: How to attract money. Let me ask you, are you trying to attract money?

J: Yes.

F: How long have you been trying to do that?

J: Last few years.

F: Has it been difficult to attract or make more money? Is that what you're saying?

J: Most of the time but just recently I realized you just, like you said, dig deeper and focus on what you have to do, and eventually it's going to happen. It's just a matter of how focused can you be on the subject.

F: Do you think that focus is really going to do it?

J: I think focus and just being honest with yourself, like being true to understanding how things work rather than how you were taught, makes a lot of difference. You have to go out and experience and see how things work based on reality and not based off what you learned in school and from family and friends.

F: Tell me, what have you learned about the law of attraction?

J: What I've learned about the law of attraction is if you think about something in a positive way, if you think about it, technically you can attract it just by focusing on the thing.

F: Have you been able to attract? You said you've been doing it 3 or 4 years, and it hasn't been working, right?

J: It happened, but not as much as I was expecting.

F: Why do you think you need the money?

J: First, it's to be independent, and financial security, which is one of the most important needs that every human being has. Financial security will also enable me not to worry about having to work for a company or work for anyone. I've always wanted to work for myself and be independent and do what I want in life. To enjoy life, and not worry if I don't have enough money to do what I want.

F: Do you think that having money is one of the most important things in life?

J: No, I think having peace of mind and being happy is most important.

F: Do you want the money, so that you can have peace of mind?

J: I'm not sure actually.

F: Well think about it.

J: Alright. Well technically the way we were raised.

F: You were still raised somewhere else. You came here as an adult.

J: I think it's coming from society pretty much.

F: When do you think was the first time you heard about money bringing peace of mind?

J: Probably from my family. Just randomly through conversations we were having.

F: How old do you think you were the first time you heard it?

J: Maybe like 9 years-old.

F: During that time, was anyone having a hard time with money?

J: Not at that time, not really, but my parents were always busy working.

F: It was important for them to be able to provide, right?

J: Yes, especially my dad. My mom didn't work most of the time, she was most of the time raising the kids.

F: Was she working sporadically in between?

J: Yes.

F: Was dad the main breadwinner?

J: Yes.

F: Was he always worried?

J: He was always pressured.

F: Was he transferring that pressure into the household members?

J: Yes.

F: What things would he say in the house, things you remember, that have just stayed in your mind until now?

J: It was mostly arguments with my mom, and we would hear them.

F: Were you able to hear them argue about money? What would they say?

J: They would be arguing and he would mention that he helps a lot with money and vacations. My mom would take vacations. Every year she would go to

Egypt or Europe, and she would go for like 2-3 months at a time. She would take all of us, while he would be busy doing his own thing, every summer pretty much. Usually he would always call to see what she's doing and she didn't like that. So, they would just argue. Things like "I paid for this", and "I paid for that".

F: Did you hear your dad talk about that?

J: Pretty much yeah. The main issue was trust, like they had trust issues. The problem wasn't really money. It was mostly trust issues. He was in a band before. He was a musician. He was a famous musician. I guess at that time a lot of girls were talking to him. They would come to him during a concert. They didn't have cell phones back then and he would be driving his car, his window would be open, and he would receive letters and stuff like that. Anyways, so mostly arguments about trust. He would think that she's cheating on him, and she did know that he was cheating on her. They would just bring up during the argument, like "I paid for this" and "I paid for that".

F: Was there resentment?

J: Yeah and she would be like "I wasted my time with you".

F: When you were hearing this, did you think money must be very important?

J: I thought money was important. Technically in my culture, they don't teach you that as much. I learned that mostly when I came here because I was independent, when I came to the U.S. At first, I was getting a lot of support, but once I decided to just stay here, they were going through a divorce, and I guess they just started taking care of their own. I just stopped asking for help, and I started working for myself.

F: What did it feel like when you couldn't ask for help, and you had to start on your own?

J: It felt really tough.

F: Scary?

J: It felt scary, yeah.

F: Were you able to sleep at night or were you constantly worried?

J: I was worried and it made me not be able to sleep, because it was new to me. I wasn't used to that. I had to learn how to deal with it, but by the time I learned to deal with it, I already messed up with my school, messed up with a lot of things.

F: How did you mess up?

J: I couldn't focus on anything because I was always worried about needing to have money to pay rent, pay my car, pay my gas, food, all the things that you need.

F: And you didn't have support, correct?

J: There was no support after my parents' divorce.

F: How old were you?

J: That happened before I got married; I was probably 22.

F: And prior to that point, in your culture parents usually help their kids, right?

J: Yeah, I was used to being taken care of.

F: Even when parents had financial difficulties, do they still take care of their children?

J: Yeah, I didn't expect it to change when it did.

F: When you got married, were you still scared about finances?

J: I was actually terrified because at that time Kelly had just started working, but the company moved to a different state and they fired everyone. So, she was laid off for the first time, and she was always working but that was the first time she was laid off. I spent a few years being the only one working at that time, and I had to work extra hard to provide for both of us. I was also going through the immigration process, and I needed a lot of extra money to keep us going, get our own apartment and all that stuff. It was tough. It wasn't easy. It caused a lot of issues with me and her as well.

F: Do you think a part of you, in the back of your head, was always worried about money?

J: Pretty much.

F: How does that affect you when you want to buy something, or you want to go out?

J: It makes me think if I should spend or save.

F: Are you able to save money?

J: Not really.

F: Basically it makes you think whether you should spend or not, right?

J: Right.

F: Do you and your spouse argue about how to spend money?

J: At the beginning. The first few years of marriage, but now were both are working and we both have our own things. I pretty much assisted Kelly to go over finances and budget until we get used to it. Now for the last few months it's been good.

F: Your marriage was basically what you saw your parents experience, arguing over money. History was repeating itself, right?

J: Pretty much.

F: Have you heard about the law of attraction?

J: Yes.

F: What is the law of attraction from your view point?

<u>J</u>: It's pretty much, what you think of can happen, and you can attract. Like if you are negative, you can attract negativity. If you're thinking positive, you can attract positive things.

<u>F</u>: When you want to think positive about having money, how do you think positively about money?

<u>J</u>: I don't think about money directly. I think about what's going to make money. I think about my business. I think about the strategy, and building a system that I know works. I've tried it before, just following and executing the system, and everything falls into place.

<u>F</u>: What steps do you take, in order for your business to grow?

<u>J</u>: When business gets slow, it just makes me wake up and try to think about what the issue is. I try to find the issue, why it's slowing down, but if it's based on the market, there's nothing I can do. I just focus on other things. I try and improve right away. I don't want to wait until the last minute because I would just go broke with nothing. It brings some sort of fear, but I don't wait until the whole business collapses. It just makes me more alert to go out there and try and find a solution for it.

<u>F</u>: You focus more on an action. You go out and try and find a solution, correct?

<u>J</u>: Yes.

<u>F</u>: Do you still fear of not having money?

J: Yeah.

F: Can you see how having fear causes your fear to build up even more?

J: Yes.

F: When you tell yourself to focus, what do you focus on?

J: To focus on the business growing.

F: What do you visualize?

J: That's a good question. I visualize ... I'm visualizing on what kind of improvement I need, but sometimes I end up thinking negatively because I start thinking about the problem. So, you're right about that. I'm visualizing the problem that we're having.

F: Do you think even though you're thinking positive, what is inside of you may prevent that, because you're also giving negative energy that you're not even aware of?

J: Yeah, because of what I've been through.

F: How do you think we could get rid of that so that you can go forward?

J: Probably start a new page, and if there is any negativity or people that are bringing negative energy, that are not good for business, just cut them off, and focus on bringing good energy to the business.

<u>F:</u> You said when you were a kid you could hear your parents arguing over money. Now turn to your relationship. Can you see that dichotomy again? What do you see?

<u>J:</u> I realized this is coming from my childhood.

<u>F:</u> Seeing yourself, reliving your parents arguing, right?

<u>J:</u> I am realizing it was not just with money but trust issues, just exactly the way my dad was talking to my mom. I also started talking to her in that way sometimes. In the past, not now.

<u>F:</u> You realized you were repeating what you experienced, right? Now you're being your dad and she's being your mom - so how does this realization make you feel?

<u>J:</u> If I don't stop that immediately I'm going to be a loser.

<u>F:</u> Or divorced like your parents, right?

<u>J:</u> Yeah.

<u>F:</u> And you don't want that?

<u>J:</u> Yeah.

<u>F:</u> You said that the way you were talking with your wife changed a few months ago. How did you change that?

J: Well it went to a point, for a couple years, where I almost got a divorce a few times. We both felt really bad because we worked very hard to achieve what we had achieved, and we realized we could lose everything and then we reconciled. We got back together and talked about it, and then agreed not to argue, but just to focus on what we can improve and if that didn't work out and we're unhappy, then we can just move on. We worked on focusing on the priorities, so we wrote down priorities and we followed it and whenever we had arguments we tried to remember to not escalate it and just focus on the priorities.

F: By focusing on other priorities

J: We try to not escalate the problem.

F: And the problem is there.

J: The problem is there but it's gotten better. I don't know why it did get better but it did.

F: Are you guys sharing the information now, the same way you used to?

J: Yeah.

F: Does anybody budget?

J: Yes, we stick to the budget. Mainly because we stick to the plan, and also, we had some trust issues as well that we just we left it.

F: Why do you think it's getting better?

J: For the trust issues, we just decided we're not going to talk about it, and if she ever wanted to talk to anyone else then she can do that. She ended up not talking to anyone else, and we got back together and moved on I guess.

F: You decided to not act up from your fear or resentment of her talking to someone else. Were you afraid you were going to lose her?

J: Yeah

F: And it just ended up happening that she didn't talk to anyone else?

J: It happened before we got married, and she did talk to someone, and then she wanted to be with someone else. I told her that's fine. I also wanted to be single at that time too. So we experienced this in the past and now we know if we ever do not want to be together, we have the option. It was mainly about the budget because I was working, she wasn't working.

F: The budget placed a stress on your relationship, is that what you say?

J: I was pressured to cover for everything, and when she wanted to talk to other guys I felt like I was being used.

F: So, you were paying for everything, you were being your dad?

J: *laughter*

F: Was it the talking that was bothering you or it was just having a relationship with somebody?

J: Having a relationship or dating or trying to date.

F: Was she trying to date other people when she was with you, is that what you are saying?

J: Yes.

F: Was it like dating other guys or just being a friend, because there is a difference?

J: Some were just friends. Some she was trying to date.

F: She was trying to date while she was with you, and you didn't like that, right?

J: Yeah and some she did date; she went out behind my back. She didn't want to say anything because she didn't want to lose me at that time, and she wasn't sure if it was going to work out with her new relationship. That's why I talked about budget, I was just saying don't use my money to be with other guys.

F: Does your wife want an open relationship?

J: She wanted that but not anymore, I guess.

F: You didn't want an open relationship, is that what you are saying?

J: I didn't want an open relationship, if I was being responsible for everything.

F: Well it's not just money, right? Culturally, it's not something you would want, right?

J: Yeah exactly.

F: For you, having your wife means a lot correct?

J: Yes.

F: When you have a wife, do you think you two are committed to each other?

J: That is correct.

F: You come from a Muslim background correct?

J: Correct.

F: So, as a Muslim, a wife and husband - they just don't cheat on each other. Men sometimes do it but it's not acceptable for the woman to do that right?

J: Yes, that's true.

F: So, it was a big step for you to even tell her she can date if she wants to, correct?

J: Yes.

F: How did you see it?

J: Yeah, I just went through a lot when I stopped getting support so I had no option but to do the right thing, and I thought this was the right thing because if I'm going to hold her back it's not going to fix itself.

F: What do you mean by when you stopped getting support?

J: When I stop getting financial support from the family, I had to figure out a way to make money on my own, and I didn't have time to worry about things that do not make me succeed, which is arguing about whether we should be together or whether she shouldn't date other people. I changed my priorities pretty much. It came down to focus on work. Focus on being independent, and if she's not going to want to be with me that's fine. She can just be with someone else.

F: You can't really prioritize your love and your wife.

J: Yeah, I couldn't prioritize anyone.

F: So how did you accept it? You still haven't answered because you know that's not the answer.

J: *Laughter*

F: It's okay.

J: I just thought maybe…

F: Were you scared to lose her?

J: Well, yeah.

F: Yeah, did you think that if you don't agree, then she's going to walk out, and you won't even have her?

J: I didn't want to lose my relationship with her, but I also wanted to have peace of mind. I didn't want her to be where she wasn't happy. When things happened, I felt betrayed, and then when you feel betrayed you are just going to hate the person. I guess because of the hate, the love is not the same anymore, at that time. Now it's different. It's changed again. I guess I stopped loving her as much as I did, and then I just decided to focus on myself.

F: You decided whether it works or not, it's okay. You're not investing in the relationship, you both are just going to go on and mind your own business, right?

J: I left like it's out of my control. If I'm going to try to stop her it's only going to cause more problems.

F: So, you decided that this is the safer bet, and you didn't really invest in this anymore. This is going to be good for now, and you're enjoying yourself.

J: Yeah.

F: At what point did that change?

J: Like when?

F: You said that the relationship changed, when?

J: It changed just recently, a few months ago.

F: How did it change?

J: Well we started off as just being friends again, even though we were married.

F: And you didn't really have a relationship, right?

J: Our relationship was drifting apart. We decided to give each other some space. We're just going to be friends again, have teamwork and whatever happens later happens. She is free to date whoever she wants, and she said I was free to date, even though I know she wouldn't let me date anyone.

F: Why do you think she was telling you that when she doesn't want you to date others?

J: I felt she has some sort of power over me because she was helping me with the green card.

F: And you think she was holding that over you?

J: She was. She actually threatened me about it when she wasn't working for 2 years. For the whole two years I was paying for her car, my car, her rent, like everything, just like the guy. I come from the Middle East - we pay for everything. When she tried dating other guys, I got into an argument with her because of it but it wasn't like a regular argument; it escalated because she started threatening me with my legal status which has nothing to do with her. I loved her so I really did not know how to react to that.

F: So, you got scared because you thought it could influence your livelihood?

J: I felt it could have an impact.

F: So, you decided to just be friends and let it go. This person is not going to be the mother of your child.

J: Yes. It didn't come off easy, she didn't come to me and say that "I want to date other people. I know you've been helping with everything but we're not going to work out being together". She just started dating other people. Bottom line, I just felt betrayed. I felt like that's not the person I love. I didn't expect it from her because she's never done that. We've been together for a long time. I was upset that she was seeing other people, and I wanted to just feel like I'm not wasting my time with someone that I'm not going to be with, and invest in someone that I'm going to be with eventually.

F: Why do you think you got into a relationship with someone that has the same dichotomy as your parents?

J: I'm not sure.

F: Well you do see that right?

J: Yeah

F: Did your mom have a relationship with other people as far as you know?

J: I haven't seen any but I heard her speaking with some guys I guess.

F: Culturally that was not good, right?

J: Yeah, and I thought most likely it was either the way she was raised as well, or that my dad wasn't giving her enough attention.

F: There are similarities, right?

J: I think the way I was raised. Like you said we can talk to a lot of girls, and I guess in the environment I was in, usually guys talk to a lot of girls. If a guy is married, he could have girlfriends on the side. Maybe that had an impact, some impact on me, that when I came here, I was talking to a few girls or at least I liked to go out on weekends with my friends and meet new people. Even if I was in a relationship, I still would go out to meet girls and talk to them. That only happened until I was maybe 22; then when I got married, I was focused on work. I had no chance to do anything.

F: Up to age 22, you were just having relationships with girls, and when you got married you stopped doing it because you wanted to be faithful?

J: Yes, and we met when I was 20. She was 19, I was 20.

F: What do you think attracted that same dichotomy of having a trust issues?

J: I'm not sure. I mean it would most likely start with my dad, because he had the same story. He was talking to a lot of girls in front of us too, and even though he told us to not to do that we just saw him, like we would hear him on the phone with girls.

F: Is it fair to say that when you were in a relationship, you thought well "Something is going to give" when you never really had trust towards another woman?

J: Yes.

F: Even when you met Kelly, you really didn't think she would be faithful to you?

J: Not with Kelly. Well, actually maybe at the beginning but once I got to know her … at first, she was always in love with me. I've always known that she was faithful but I don't know.

F: But do you think it hurt her to see you not being faithful when you were boyfriend and girlfriend?

J: Yeah.

F: Are Kelly's parents together and trust each other?

J: I think they have some trust issues too.

F: Did you ever really think that you would have a wife who would not cheat on you?

J: I've always felt like anything can happen. I thought it could happen, yeah.

F: You didn't really think that you could marry someone and fully trust them not to cheat on you?

J: Yeah.

F: Do you see how you've attracted that because of your thought process? You already thought that you're not going to have a faithful relationship.

J: Right.

F: You entered into a relationship knowing that you're not going to be faithful, right?

J: Yes.

F: Because you weren't. You just changed your way because you were in love. You both attracted it.

J: Right.

F: You just found something that you never thought about. Now you know that you've attracted that in your life.

J: Right.

F: And you were surprised that things were going a way you didn't want them to go, right?

J: Yeah.

F: It's a belief system that was put in place by your parents, through the fighting dichotomy that they had. That they can't trust each other. You didn't anticipate anything beyond that because that was your model. You emulate their thought process, their belief system as your own. In order for you to have a good relationship, you have to get rid of that belief system and believe that there could be a good relationship with faithfulness and trust.

J: I do believe that because I see a lot of people that never worry about trust.

F: And you were asking this question in your head because you had the lack of trust. So now that you know where it's coming from, you need to understand yourself that when a woman is going to be with you, it's not for your money, and she loves you. The fact that you think otherwise is because of your lack of love towards yourself. You don't see yourself as worthy, worthy of their trust.

J: True.

F: That's why you accepted her dating other people.

J: Right.

F: Work on finding yourself worthy. After finding yourself complete, see that there's nothing wrong with you and you are loveable.

J: Yeah.

F: It starts by you recognizing you and then when somebody comes to you, you're not surprised that they love you. You don't think they want something from you. You don't think that it's going to be just for a short term.

J: True.

F: You are a good person, and when others find who you are, they're going to love you.

J: Right, I am not hiding anything.

F: You just be. So, that's the state when you are yourself and you are present with your authentic self. You can't get there until you actually first get to know you. You have a lot of little holes in you that were created since childhood. Those holes were things you heard and you adopted them. Once you get rid of those holes, you will feel better about yourself. Most of them are from you not seeing yourself being worthy of trust and love. When you get rid of those little holes, then you can enter into a relationship knowing that you deserve to get into a good relationship because you offer a good relationship. Then you don't have to worry about them being unworthy of trust because you already found a partner who's like you.

J: Right.

F: Your thought process becomes that you don't need to look for anybody else because you are complete, and you end up meeting someone who is complementing you. Change the way you think.

J: You have to change the way you think?

F: Change the way you think about yourself.

J: About myself?

F: If you don't love yourself, you're going to constantly think that you are not a good package.

J: And they will feel the same thing.

F: We receive other people's projection; the way you treat people, the way you talk, then you, in turn, give that vibe to them too.

J: You're right.

F: Once you start working on you, like your focus on lack of money, you just have to figure out where that fear comes from and get rid of it, and then you attract things because you don't have that fear in you anymore, you don't project that fear.

J: Then you are not afraid of doing big things, that you thought couldn't get done.

F: Because then you know yourself and that you can do it, but only when you know who you are.

J: Right, that's true.

F: And then you're going to have a support system from people you know because they know you, and "you" are a complete person. They can count on you, because you are counting on yourself.

J: That's true, you can visualize what you can put yourself into.

F: You don't have to have those fears anymore because you already resolved them. What we just had was a conversation, and you can have that conversation with yourself and say. "Hey where is that coming from", see for yourself. You can find out what you don't like, and then when you look at it, you realize it's other people's perceptions, and you don't have to accept it from other people. There's nothing wrong with you, you are whole. You don't have any deficiency. You don't have any inadequacy. It's what you put in your head, and what other people put in your head.

J: Thank you so much.

Conversation between George from Mexico & Faith

October 27, 2017: Faith is lost on her way back home from Tijuana, Mexico. She finally finds her way to San Ysidro border and finds herself in the regular border crossing road instead of the Real Lane for American. Where cars are lined up, many Mexican nationals are engaged in attempting to sell their goods to people departing Mexico. There are many peddlers, beggars, and sellers of goods, food and sweets. Parents with children are trying to sell their goods to travelers.

I am wondering how did I end up in a regular lane for border crossing. I see four Mexican men, each selling something to passengers willing to pay. I open my window and they all walk towards my vehicle. I ask where is the Real Lane for American.

The fourth person steps forward and says, "Let me show you. You need to let me drive your car to show you."

I am looking at him, puzzled and pondering giving my keys to a stranger.

The other says, "He is a family man and has kids. He is ok and will show you the way to help you."

I hesitate for a moment and acknowledge to myself that my hesitation is from my habit of not trusting strangers and peddlers. I smile and get out of the driver's seat and sit in the back seat. I realize my car door can be locked from the front and contemplate for a second whether I should sit next to the driver's seat.

Again, I acknowledge my habit from what I learned all my life. I sit in the back seat. I trust my intuition. George starts backing up the car for a long time toward what I call the freeway or main road to the border crossing. Then, he takes an exit to the left and we enter the City again. He drives and we talk.

I ask George whether he is always at the border and George starts asking me questions. George asks where is my husband. I respond I am divorced. George asks if I have any kids? I respond, one, a girl age 7. George asks whether I have a boyfriend or like Mexican men. I respond with a smile that I am ok and currently am not looking for a boyfriend. He asks again whether I like Mexican men.

I respond, "I've never contemplated that, but I am not currently looking for a boyfriend." George asks why.

I respond, "I am taking a break and I am happy."

George looks at me intently.

I smile again and said, "I am happy."

George asks, "Do you like to dance?" I respond that I do.

George asks if I wanted to go dancing. I respond that I only like to dance with my girl. George asks "Where?" I tell him we dance at our home. George asks about why don't I go dancing. I responded with, "I am happy where I am. I do not feel the need."

Then, we started talking about his kid and his commerce. We pass a police car and I then noticed we have been now driving for a few minutes and he is turning into the side streets. Habits kick in as I recall for a moment multiple movies always showing a woman kidnapped by her own stupidity and the streets looked like these.

I say to George, "We have been driving for a while and I see all these streets and alleys -- where are we going? The Real Lane was next to the other lane I was when I saw you."

George responds, "You saw the police car -- don't be afraid."

I checked myself. I checked my feeling and felt no fear. I noticed my hands; they were holding themselves and I see that as a serious concern, but I had no feelings of fear. I check myself again, and I recognized for one moment that I have concern and mistrust him.

George, looking at me intently, says, "No worry, I will get you to the border."

I felt tears collecting in my eyes. I felt compassion for myself and him.

I tell George, "You are a good man. I know I am ok with you. Thank you so much for taking me to the border. You must be working and you are here. Thank you."

George says, "You will take care of me."

I smile and say, "I will surely thank you."

George drives and we finally get to Real Lane. George tells me he will continue driving until we get closer and then he will get out.

I see a small child about age 3 with her father selling goods for $1. It is very hot and the kid looks thirsty. The father is placing her in front of himself to sell. I am looking at the little girl and ask for my open purse next to George by the driver's seat. George hands it to me. I know I only have $100 bills. I take a $100 bill and hand it to the little girl. The father takes it. The little girl tries to give me the sweet. I smile and said "Keep it and thank you."

I am still moved. I see a handicapped man with one leg and a small boy age 3 or 4. This child is happy and content and eating one of the candies they sell. The father stops and kisses the boy with affection. I take another $100 and open the window and hand it to the disabled man. George stops, gets up, and says he is now where he could walk. I get up, gave him a hug, and thanked him for his kindness.

Again, I said, "You are a very good man." I hand him $100 and say I hope you accept this. George was happy.

I used to lock my car doors from inside. I would have never handed my keys to any stranger, let alone in another country to a person I could not communicate with well and could not even speak the language in that country. That was my programming, but I no longer had the same programming. I had no fear and what I saw was my body's reactions and reflexes out of habit. I saw myself and I saw my body reacting when my emotions appeared to be steady with no signs of fear (as I could not detect any).

Conversation with Sherry

Sherry is an American living in Israel. Her parents were holocaust survivors. She has a bachelor's degree and runs her own business.

<u>Sherry:</u> I feel my Dharma is to build this export business in Israel and make it a success. I feel I am meant to come here and to do this. This is my Dharma. I want to build this successful business and make money to have everything I want. This will give me the freedom I want.

<u>Faith:</u> There is no Dharma. That is another terminology from another belief system that you have adapted. You can keep adapting it if you want, but it won't serve you. Building a business is empowering you to acknowledge you as the powerful being that you are. That is your lesson. Wanting money is feeding the need that you have within you. It is also a part of your belief system since childhood where you learned that money is important. You feel that money can fill the gap within and it will cure your problems or unhappiness from feeling unfulfilled and incomplete. Once you have money, you will realize you still feel unfulfilled and incomplete. You will continue to work towards keeping the money, because to lose it would be terrifying to you, or make more of the same because the loss of it is horrifying to you and you still feel you can fill the gap with more.

Money is another distraction with no value, except what you associated it with. The power of money is in the collective thought process, giving it energy. The important thing is how building the business helps you to know yourself again, trust yourself, and feel whole again.

Abundance is not about having money. Abundance is the state of fulfillment felt in every fiber of your being with no polarity.

S: I don't want to over-analyze. I am trying to follow my intuition. On one hand I want to be happy and on the other hand there is this urge to do certain things. I do not know if that is ego or actually me or my soul wanting to do these things. I feel inadequacies about trying to prove to myself to everyone that I am good enough.

I understand about inadequacies and I felt that especially with my father. I always wanted to prove to myself that I am good enough or I am smart enough or I deserve or whatever. I always felt from my father that his expectations of me were very low. He did not expect much from me. I picked up on the fact that my dad had low expectation of me and all my life I am trying to prove to myself that I am not undeserving and I am someone who can succeed. It is weird to look at your parent's face and feel that. Because I was abused as a child by my mom, if I said one word, my mom would have hit me or put me in the closet. I have been searching and I am still not sure if I know who I really am because of all the stuff that I am going through in this particular lifetime. There is a kind of belief within me - could be subconscious - that tells me something positive about me, but the true self that I am, I am not sure who that is. I am trying to be a good mother, wife and daughter and good to everyone else. Everyone's needs come first and my needs comes last and I am trying to make everyone happy. I am trying to follow my intuition and my feelings. I am trying to find my path. Sometimes I am so proud of myself for building this business but sometimes I want to be back home, in Los Angeles.

F: You touched on a lot of issues. You see how your past and behavior of others and their perceptions set a belief system within you. You are realizing that and making efforts to erode and erase it from you because you know that your inner self knows you are complete. You know you do not need anyone's approval. You are aware and you are able to detect. Whether your dad was projecting that onto you is immaterial; it is what you perceived it to me. Your dad may or may not have had that feeling. He could have projected that through his frustration and you accepted that to be true. Because it came from your parent, you easily adopt it, especially since it is from someone you love and want their approval. When we adopt a belief system that goes against our core, it leaves a scar. Some people call it defragmentation or other names but it is how you scar yourself. In order to repair it, you have to acknowledge it. The reality is that you do not know what your dad was thinking. You only saw his projection of daily life's frustrations or resentments - you accepted his frustration and assumed that to be you and you owned it and accepted it. By owing it, you carried it in life and as an adult, you now strive to prove yourself. Until you get rid of that belief and accept that you do not need to prove to anyone anything and you are complete by yourself, you will continue this trend. Your whole being wants you to realize that you are whole through your experiences. This is the way for you to repair your belief system, pain, scar within you. Now as an adult, you realize that through your efforts that you are doing great but a part of you still seeking approval. You want evidence of your empowerment and what you are capable of doing. The state of fulfillment is a state where you do not need to prove anything to anyone because it is a state of power. Once you are aware of that core level, shifts start happening. Whether you are here or in another country, it is geography.

S: How do we know who we really are?

F: You are a soul. You play a role in this Virtual Reality through your experiences or distractions to get back to who you are.

S: Basically everything is distractions. Bottom line is that we are just the soul and pure love and contentment and joy, if we just get back to our true self.

F: Yes, and everything is distractions. The way we grow up, religion, condition, circumstances in this physical world - it takes us away from realizing our true self. We went through many lives and the purpose for you and I and everyone is to see through the distractions.

S: That is such a basic idea.

F: Yes.

S: It is so basic that it seems that it can't be.

<u>F</u>: It is simple. All needs and wants are distractions. Every title or position or desire comes from a need or want.

<u>S</u>: That is ego, right?

<u>F</u>: Ego has a lot to do with how we maneuver through our lives but also it is a part of the belief systems that we feed to ourselves with distractions that we create and strings that we attached to ourselves.

<u>S</u>: I think it is ego. If I do not care about my business, if I do not care whether I succeed or not, if I just go there every day and whatever happens, happens...the feeling of wanting to succeed and be successful has to be ego.

<u>F</u>: There is a misunderstanding. I am not saying to disregard your efforts. I am not saying not to be successful. You are seeking to make this business a success because it empowers you. You can see the fruit of your labor. You can see what you are able to do as a human being. This makes you excited. It makes you feel good about yourself. There is nothing wrong with that.

<u>S</u>. Isn't that ego?

<u>F</u>: Ego is a part of our nature in this physical world. That is what guides distraction. To have no ego, you have no distraction. Let's look at a business as being a wall that you build but it is a wall that you want to climb over. Despite efforts to climb up, you need to celebrate and acknowledge to yourself that you did that. It is great that you set out to do it. I am not saying to disregard your efforts. If the business was

a wall or a distraction, you built it because you want to climb it and cross over for your own reasons that you set for yourself in this life. By doing that, you recognize that you are a powerful being. You can call it ego. We need the ego. Too much ego is not good but we need certain amount to progress; otherwise, your drive will be lost.

S: I need to convince myself that I built the wall, reached and climbed the wall in the U.S. and obviously, I did not feel that I did it alone or it was not good enough, so I re-created another wall or job for myself here.

F: It is about acknowledging you are a powerful being. If you still think you are not good enough or you are inadequate, then you do not see yourself as you should.

S: I see very clearly now. I feel proud of myself for my accomplishment and what I have done.

F: Do you feel it in your heart?

S: When I see the warehouse, customers and orders ready to go to a store, I feel very proud of it. I do also recognize the fact that I have this stupid need to continue to prove to others that I am what I am. I do not know why.

F: That is part of your program and belief system that you are only as good as others recognize in you. No one outside of you can complete you or make you feel good about yourself.

S: I recognize the fact that I have a need to care more for what other people thought about me.

F: This has to do with a belief system. You have a religious, cultural background - a collective consciousness or belief system.

S: Let me tell you about the Jewish thing. I was not raised in a regular Jewish family. I had no idea about the Bible. My dad grew up with it but my mom grew up as a Catholic. In my home, we did traditional stuff. If we had a Christmas tree, we had Hanukah. What does Hanukkah mean? I do Rash Hashanah and I do all these things because we get together. Shabbat is to get together and have meal together. For me there is absolutely no religion in my Jewishness.

F: I am saying the thought process of being successful. You mentioned in our last talk that you are Jewish, and there is an expectation to be successful.

S: I was saying that I was noticing that other people's perception of Jewish people is that they all have money and control Hollywood. That to me was the weirdest thing. I remember this neighbor saying all Jewish people are smart and have all the money. I said the Carnegies, Kennedys, Vanderbilts are not Jewish. There are many non-Jewish people who have so much money and none are Jewish. I found that interesting

F: That is his perception and it is projected.

S: Obviously. I heard these things before but never in my face and the neighbor thought he was politically correct.

F: Why did your neighbor's statement hurt you?

S: Because it is not true, the families I mentioned, none are Jewish and are the richest families in America and built the roads and banks; you name it, they built it.

F: Why does it bother you in particular?

S: I felt insulted.

F: Why?

S: For throwing all of us into one stereotype.

F: What do you mean by all of us?

S: All the Jews.

F: You identify with the religion?

S: Not with the religion. I identify myself with the Jewish people. Being Jewish is important to me. I identify myself as Jewish. My parents were Holocaust survivors.

F: The thought process is that you separate yourself from consciousness of Jewish people because you do not practice religion per se, but identify with them, and accept their collective consciousness to the extent you think it is ok for you to accept. The part that you feel is too religious, you say you do not accept it. Because you identify with collective consciousness, you identify yourself with being a Jewish. The same with a Muslim, identifying themselves as being Muslim or a Christian identifying with being Christian. What he said, he was separating himself and you, did the same. It is subconsciously done and it goes under the radar. You adapt the belief system from the religion. I do not identify myself with being Muslim. If someone says something unkind about Muslims, I do not get offended. I may say that there are good and bad people. The same with Christian and Jewish people. Because I have come to terms with religion as collective consciousness.

S: It is ridiculous and he says Jewish people are successful and I was insulted by that.

F: He says Jewish people are successful and there are people who have less. You see insult because your collective consciousness is attached to a certain belief system. Analyze why you think the comments were insulting. This was a good subject and it shows how we identify ourselves through our religion and separate ourselves from our religion.

S: I still have problems seeing it. I am talking about it and have trouble seeing it. My neighbor is American and so am I. We both are in the Middle East and I accept that I identify myself with Jewish people and I am not seeing myself Jewish because of so many factions. The way people think here and do, are stuff that I do not relate to.

F: Let's look at what the neighbor said. He thought Jewish people are very successful. Why did that sentence bother you?

S: I felt he was stereotyping all of us.

F: What is the stereotype? Define it.

S: That we are successful and we are ...I don't know. I felt insulted that the neighbor is putting all of us in one basket. Maybe I feel guilty about being successful. I do not know where it is coming from.

F: Sometimes, our own barrier, in an effort to protect us, does not let us see it. Let's look into it. You got insulted. Why did you feel insulted that all Jewish people are successful? Where does that come from? When did you hear that the first time?

S: I do not know.

F: It probably comes from a long time ago. As a child, did you ever feel that you are looked at differently as a Jewish child?

S: Yes, I heard that when I was little. My dad was explaining to me that we are Jews, and we are the chosen people. I did not understand and asked him what he was talking about. He explained that we are chosen by God and are more special, but that had nothing to do with money or success.

F: You are saying that you understood that Jewish people are special among the rest?

S: Yes.

F: You do know every religion says the same? At what point did you hear people's view of Jewish people as insulting about money?

S: I do not know. I think because my parents were Holocaust survivors and growing up with my dad, he used to say, do not attract attention to yourself, do not show to people that you are successful and fly under the radar and hide your star.

F: Why was he saying that?

S: Because he did not want me to get hurt and attacked since that was what happened in Europe. Rich Jews were the first one sent to death camps.

F: But your dad was in the U.S. and there was no threat here, and he was delivering his belief system.

S: Of course. It is because he had such a horrible experience in Europe.

F: He was teaching you his belief system, while no Jewish was being prosecuted in America. So, you identify yourself as vulnerable? As a special group of people?

S: Yes, I was already scared since my mother was so abusive. I used to tell myself don't say anything or do anything so you won't get beaten up. Sit quiet and play in a corner. I was terrified of her. That was already inside of me as a child, to fly under the radar about being Jewish. Being Jewish was just another layer since I was already doing that with surviving the abuse in my own home.

F: When the neighbor said Jewish people are successful and you felt insulted. That is the root of how you identify yourself in relation to money. When do you think you felt that having money and being Jewish was unwelcomed if others noticed?

S: I do not remember when.

F: Where you a little girl?

S: I do not remember when. I just remember thinking that if someone is going to see that I am rich and successful or rich and Jewish, I might be in danger because of what my parents told me. I do not remember when it happened. I remember I felt a shiver went down my spine and all of a sudden, I felt I should feel guilty and ashamed to be Jewish and wealthy.

F: But your reaction was not shame. It was lashing out at your neighbor.

S: My reaction was anger. I was angry. I did not like what my neighbor said. I felt he was racist because he was equating (all Jews) with being rich. Maybe that was my perception when I was growing up. Maybe I was surrounded with successful people but we flew under the radar.

F: When the neighbor said that to you, did you feel how dare you? Maybe I am entitled to it since we work hard. Where do you think that resentment or anger came from when he said that to you?

S: I do not know.

F: Do you realize that his comments are not insulting but it is merely his perception?

S: Yes, his perception pissed me off because it was stereotype and I was extremely insulted by it.

F: Finding out could also answer your relationship with money and success. We could do this but I do not want you to be frustrated. The purpose is to calmly detect yourself and go back. What he said triggered a belief system from the past about Jewish people and the relationship with money and other people's judgements or perceptions of your identity as a Jewish person.

S: I think his perception of Jews really bothered me. It is so interesting that all the stuff we are thought as a kid, we accept. The whole idea of just being the being and all the rest is just what it is to teach and expand. Now I have the awareness and I know I am who I really am. My soul, my being. It is not this individual, the suit or body that I am using here.

F: Once you fully embrace that, nothing bothers you when someone says that Jewish people are successful, it does not matter.

S: Right and it did. Other things about my life that bothers me is to be a good mother and a good wife.

F: Now that you are aware, you acknowledge it and start exploring where it comes from.

S: Yes, but it was a very strong feeling and wanting. I am recognizing it and looking at it right in the face, and I see now that it is a part of this game. There is a need to succeed and the ambition to succeed.

F: Nothing wrong with it. That ambition helps you to repair all trauma you went through by not recognizing and feeling inadequate, not worthy, not loved, not supported and it teaches you to overcome.

S: When I look at myself in the mirror, I recognize it. I am ok with me. I am a good person.

F: Every day is a new experience and a new lesson.

S: This goes back to purpose. If there is no purpose then we are here to understand or remember to be just fulfilled, happy and joyful and understanding of our being and accepting who we are. Every day is a journey and experience like traveling and seeing new places and things. Coming down to have a good time.

F: Just being. Enjoying what you have because it is an experience. To accomplish that you tackle limiting belief systems. You have been reincarnated multiple times and each time you had a different religion, color, gender and creed. The religion is important to you because as you said, you identify with it and this is what you were taught from childhood. A Muslim child learns about Islam. A Christian child learns about Christianity. A Hindu child learns about Hinduism. Being a Holocaust victim means you identify yourself with the victims.

We act as what we think we are and identify ourselves with. This is all a part of building layers and burying ourselves in our belief system because it feeds our need to belong. Being Jewish separates you from others. It is a form of conditioning since birth and it creates separation.

Conversation with Alex

Alex is in his early 20's, and has graduated from University with a Bachelor of Science in Philosophy.

<u>Faith</u>: What do you feel is holding you back or preventing you from achieving your goals? It may be more than one thing. Find the one thing that is the most present for you.

<u>Alex:</u> I think what holds me back the most is shame and guilt from past experiences. Even this past weekend for example, I was with some of my friends from my undergrad, and I noticed I was trying to going back to past situations and repeat them. I had to confront the belief I had, that the past should be different versus it is the way it is. This morning for example, when I woke up, I was able to see different parts of my consciousness, and I can at least see different kinds of facades or dynamics fall off, almost like an avalanche or shedding, but I saw myself looking at the past, or the people that I was close with and had fallings out with, and I could just see it. I realized I always try to understand everything, and instead of that approach, what I did was I just said, "Show me" because the reasoning doesn't matter, what matters is just that it's there and I was just looking at kind of all the past levels of consciousness fade away. I think that's one of the bigger things holding me back, and again I think that's just internalized shame from just growing up, and I always found myself in dynamics like that since being a child. Whether it was family, friends, leadership roles. Just that aspect of collectivism, of being the source for others, and then projecting their

needs and agenda onto you, and I just always thought that was my role. I'm also realizing the higher your frequency, people are drawn to that for a reason, just thinking of a universal consciousness. Just like a shark can sense blood, I've found that I had to step back and just see the social dynamics I was in.

F: Let's go back to the issue of shame. Shame and guilt, you said. Can you go back as far as you can remember? What was the incident that gave you the most shame and totally changed you?

A: I don't think there was one specific thing. I think it started happening around 7th or 8th grade. That's just when I started becoming more aware, but that's also when we moved in with my mother's boyfriend. He was a very strong narcissist, and he would set up different power struggles or situations. He was just a textbook narcissist, very high on the spectrum. So that was a lot of the dynamic that was set up. He just took out a lot of his aggression and projections on me. Not so much physical, I mean he would hit me, but just think of living with a bully who would just set up the most nonsensical conversations and situations. This was for about 6 years, every single day, every single hour. My mother on the other hand, I don't know if she's bipolar, but she's just very aggressive, explosive, and she has some manipulative tendencies, and he would manipulate her into that power struggle, and her boyfriend would just use her and my brother to gang up on me. That's probably the first period of my life where I was able to start understanding that I was experiencing shame.

F: The shame, hearing what you described, is abuse.

<u>A:</u> Yeah that was my background. I was abused as a child.

<u>F:</u> Abuse can bring a lot so let's look at when you felt ashamed of who you were. You were ashamed of being Alex, maybe it was much younger?

<u>A:</u> Well my biological father was physically abusive with my mother. I stopped seeing him when I was about in 3rd grade. There was a lot of different power struggles with both sides of my family, maternal and paternal.

<u>F:</u> Was it a struggle for custody?

<u>A:</u> Well there was a literal custody struggle, but it was also just them trying to have influence over me. On one side, you had his family who was very manipulative, angry, and bitter. They're bashing the other side and criticizing part of me since I'm related to the other side, and I would see that on both sides really. That was one thing. My mother's side of the family used to control me with fear. They demonized part of me and would say I was acting like that side, when I didn't do what they wanted. Also growing up, just not having friends, a family structure, being poor, and just kind of blank slate left there alone. I would even have teachers make fun of me. The area where I went to Elementary School in, at the time, was an older generation, so a lot of older racist, white people - not to sound racist - but that was just the dynamic at the time. They would just stare at me as if I were less.

<u>F:</u> Let's see if there's a dynamic within you for how you were raised, and how you were used as a pawn.

Now let's go back to when the shame first started. How old were you when you first started seeing your dad hit your mom?

A: I think I was maybe 5.

F: That was the first time you saw it?

A: It was around that age I'm trying to remember. I think I was in kindergarten at the time. They were never really a good couple. He would cheat on her all the time. I want to say I was around 5 or 6 when I would see all that.

F: You said he was cheating on your mom. How old were you when all of that happened, and how did you know?

A: Like 4 or 5, and my mother would tell me. That was one thing, is she would always get me involved. She would tell me "he didn't love me", "look what he's doing to me", and things like that.

F: Did your father start shaming you when you were younger?

A: I don't know; I don't think we were ever close. I think he just kind of didn't really want anything there. I remember there was even this one incident where, because I had an aunt I was close with on that side - no one else really, where I found out they got into a fight because she wanted to see me and it was my weekend to go over, and he didn't want me there. When I made the decision to stop seeing him, we didn't file anything legally, I just didn't want him in my life anymore. I think it was I got older, before I stopped seeing him, I noticed he tried to favor me over my younger brother, with trying to get my attention. I don't know why. Maybe he sensed that I was kind of leaning away from him.

F: So, your dad wasn't living with you guys, so you really didn't have much contact with him, except for when you visited him, correct?

A: He moved out at about, maybe when I was either at kindergarten or first grade, around there.

F: Your memory seems to start clearly from kindergarten?

A: Yeah.

F: So, was your mom alone during that time, while living with you and your brother?

A: Well, before kindergarten he was in the picture. I don't really remember much when I was younger. If I see pictures it seems like I'm smiling or that she tried to kind of have a good life for us emotionally. I don't really remember back to that point.

F: Could you be blocking it?

A: Maybe. I find that with time I regress more. I am unintentionally blocking it but different things will come back, and as they do I just welcome it because I know that's part of the healing process.

F: When you are going through hard times, sometimes it's easier not to remember them.

A: And that's kind of how we first initially start dealing with things, we shut them out.

F: It's a defense mechanism.

A: Yeah, my whole life, up until this year, when I realized what I was doing and the social dynamics I was putting myself into. I snapped out of it, but the role has always been kind of like a pawn for other people's agendas, whatever that agenda may be.

F: You always felt you were used?

A: Yeah.

F: How did that make you feel?

A: Alone. Again, that kind of defined what I thought was my inherent worth. The feeling of shame. As I got older, I started to realize and actually process how that was, and it just kind of made me feel like I was very selfless and other people weren't. That created a lot of tension the last few years of my life, just with friends. I would end up bending over backwards for people in my fraternity or other leadership roles, because I was again taught that was very much my role. I didn't pursue the things I had wanted or wasn't fully myself or my personality, because I was like "Okay I need to be smart and be able to put myself in a situation where I can affect organizations or others more", and so that meant sacrificing the other parts of me. I don't think that way anymore, but that was a role or cycle I was stuck in.

F: You were trying to be indispensable?

A: Yeah. Just that you have to always have a use.

F: Where did that belief system start? Thinking that you had to be useful. What age?

A: Around middle school and higher because that's when I was old enough to have started seeing that part of my identity, in terms of how my role relates to others. I'm sure it was way before though because that was always the role I started. I'm trying to think back because when you're a baby, you're a baby. At age two, you kind of start picking up more. I'm trying to remember where I was when I was 3, because 3 to 4, that's kind of getting into preschool.

F: When did you start helping mom do things, or trying to help out and be useful?

A: I think when I was about probably 3. That's when I started going to preschool. That had to be when both sides started actually talking to me, and trying to influence me. People project all the time. That's just what most people do, they project whether they're really aware of it or not. So probably around 3 or 4, is when I started seeing "Okay here's Alex" and people saying "Okay you do this, you do that".

F: You said about age 3 years old is when you realized that you needed to be useful.

A: Well I'm assuming when I was 2 or a baby. I wasn't really at that point yet.

F: You would just feel it at that age, but you said probably at that age of 3, you started feeling shame because you were trying to be useful, because you were ashamed of not being useful, or something within that parameter of guilt or shame, was involved in you trying to be something beyond what you were.

A: Yeah, I always had people try to shame me or use fear to get me to do what they want.

F: How would they do that? Give me an example. When you were young, 3 or 4 years old if you can, something they would do to make you do things, and you felt ashamed?

A: With my father's side of the family, they would more so verbally ask me to do things that were more favored towards their side, and then they would reward me, like buy me things, so I started associating what they want with positive reward.

F: Well give me an example of something they would tell you to do when you were a three-year-old child that you knew you didn't want to do. What you felt uncomfortable doing, but you were doing it because you were getting something out of it.

A: With that side, I don't really remember. I would say that was more dominant on my mother's side of the family, which is the one who ended up staying with.

F: Tell me what would they do?

A: They just kind of demonized me, because my biological father was half Salvadorian and half Guatemalan, and both those races are stereotyped to dislike each other, so they demonized that, they demonized him.

F: El Salvador and?

A: El Salvadorians, Guatemalans, and Mexicans are stereotyped to dislike each other.

F: And your dad was half Salvadorian and Guatemalan?

A: Yes, and my mom's family was a traditional Mexican family. They just kind of created fears of "Oh you're being like him" "You're being like that family", and then it would be something as simple as not going to clean, and then them saying "You're acting like him now, you're going to be like him". They used that to control me. They still tried, and then I got away for college, and I kind of cut contact.

F: You basically learned half of you wasn't good?

A: Yeah, that was very internalized.

F: That half of you felt ashamed and felt guilt, right?

A: Yeah, I was just always taught that there's something inherently wrong with me. I was taught to kind of live in constant fear, and the reward for doing what I was told, was someone letting me know "Okay now you know you don't have to be afraid."

F: What I hear is that you did not love yourself for a very long time, and you started, from what I hear, not seeing yourself since you were a little child, and that part of you was taken prisoner. It was taken prisoner and took a hold of you. So, you started developing a belief system about yourself, what you can or cannot do, but you did learn that you can, since you are an accomplished young person.

A: Yeah, I just did well when I came to college. The jobs, the mentors, I asked people things when I didn't know something, I learned. Learning to actually love myself and who I was, the first time - that probably happened summer my 3rd year, when I was an orientation leader. That was kind of like the job to have. You're social, fun, and I was kind of around a lot of fun people, and so I had a lively personality. After that, which I learned from the experience, someone I was really close to, it just kind of manipulated me a lot and then I ran for a leadership position. I didn't get it and the feedback was "Oh he's not serious". Again people dumping their projections, but I just kind of killed that side of me and became very serious and driven for the next two years. Again, I saw what was happening and this whole year I kind of took a step back.

F: You need to go back to that.

A: Yeah.

F: You need to go back to being the fun-loving one, because the side that isn't fun-loving, hardens to find love.

A: Yeah, I have an idea what you're talking about. I've gotten a lot of it back, just my individuality too. Again, it was an aspect of killing that side of me, like the aspect of collectivism, so I can put myself in a position to where I'm benefiting others, which I'm not a big fan of collectivism, just for that reason.

F: What do you mean about collectivism?

A: Needs of the whole are greater than the needs of the individual, because when you are kind of someone who is doing well and producing a lot, it puts you in that role of like a sacrificial animal.

F: Victimization, basically?

A: Yeah. But other than the difference between collectivism and an individual having collective values. I don't think collectivism gets played very correctly because I think again, it creates a group of people saying someone else is responsible for them. Then people are unaware, they project, they victimize themselves. Whereas, I'd rather encourage more personal responsibility which allows for individuals to have collective values, and what you owe is to just not harm other people, and then you just kind of elevate your frequency. You set that example, and in doing that the right people will be attracted to it and if they want to raise and elevate, then that's kind of on them.

F: You experienced a lot in your life as a young man. The experiences you had took away your self-worth, your self-love, and lack of appreciation of yourself. On top of that you were abused. You were victimized over and over again by the people who were supposed to protect and love you.

A: Yeah, when it's what you've grown up with and known your whole life, you have an issue distinguishing what abusive behavior is because that's all you've known. It actually wasn't until this past year when I realize that. Again I get so many things I just come into my inbox and I read a book on malignant and covert narcissism, and then I was like "Wait this is kind of ringing a bell", then I started distancing and getting away. I grew up abused because I just was never able to recognize it because that's what I knew my whole life.

F: Well even though you read that book and gave a label to a behavior, it's the personality of that person, and how he or she was.

A: Yeah, what matters isn't the title or label, what matters is the behavior that's happening.

F: Not having self-worth, or self-love, they projected that onto you.

A: With the mother's side of the family, I think a large thing that happened was my Grandpa died when they were young. My mom was 14, the rest were teenagers, and I see how it's had an impact on their life. It's almost like they're still waiting for a male figure to kind of come along and be there for them, and so they just never moved on from that point. I noticed they tried to project that role on me. They do that with my younger brother. That's where I think a lot of their issues came from and just a traditional Mexican immigrant family, the guy takes care of everyone and provides for everything, the girls are taken care of, now he dies and he's gone.

F: The guy is taken care of by the girls right because they have to?

A: Yeah. It's a very collective dynamic. I'm very blessed with the kind of the self-awareness that I have. There's really a big difference between practicing meditation and actually from a depth of being self-aware, almost like a grid being able to see your experiences on deep level. I think that's actually one thing that holds me back a lot to. Like my uncle said I live in my head too much and I realize that I try to understand everything all the time. I'm always just downloading information, just taking it in. It's a lot of energy. I can handle it now but it took a while to where it wasn't overwhelming. It's like being an energy center.

F: I can see, well, it's not that. It's just that you are so tuned in to get the essence, and you're so concerned that you may miss it or you're not getting it, that you lock.

A: Yeah, I think that's probably what holds me back the most, because I have that everywhere. I'll get very visionary, like I know the things I want to do will pan out, but I just get so caught up with trying.

F: We're going to talk about how you let go of your shame and guilt. You don't see yourself. Whatever inadequacy you had as a child or was imprinted or projected on you, has carried with you. To get rid of that, you first have to recognize it. You have to acknowledge that that's within you.

A: Bring it into consciousness.

F: You bring it and acknowledge it, acknowledge that you have this belief, that you have this desire to not acknowledge yourself or affirm yourself when you need to. Then when you are caught up with doing something, instead of trying to focus like you don't want to miss a word, see you're so concerned with not missing it, not messing up which is all in your head, when it comes into your head, tell yourself all is going to be okay. Don't let that thought take a hold of you.

A: Yeah, I've noticed I had that thing even with meditation for example, like an "Okay is it now, is it now is it now, when am I going to get this?" mindset.

F: There's going to be no assignment. You've got to start telling yourself that. You are still holding yourself in the prison of your belief system, that you're going to mess up. You're going to fuck up, and you're not going to be useful, and you're not going to be able to do it. You need to stop that thought process. You are going to let go of: You are not going to be able to do it right, adequately; that the bottom is always going to fall out and that you're going to fuck up somewhere. That is the guilt and shame, and also that is going to prevent you from moving forward. If you do move forward, you're so concerned if you're going to do it right, you put so much pressure on yourself, that even when you do it correctly, it looks like a mountain you're moving, when it actually is not. How can you now change that perception? When you're doing tasks, let's say you're listening, you focus intently. You don't need to focus intently, to accomplish a task. Well you have more than 5 senses but for now the 5 senses are sufficient enough for you to hear, listen, and carry on. Consider yourself perfect. Look at yourself in the mirror and acknowledge yourself as perfect. I'm going to give you something to do. It's called "I'm enough." I actually think that's powerful words. I heard somebody talking about it and it really works. Every morning tell yourself you're going to be fine, you're not going to fuck up, you're good at what you're doing, you are worthy, you are awesome. It's hard because you don't believe it, right?

A: I think our experiences can cause us to distrust ourselves.

F: Well it's more than that because you are so set in that belief system that you accepted it. You accepted other people's projections as your own about your adequacy. Now you have to unwind that. You open it up to reprogram yourself. You really have to reprogram yourself to be back to the little kid that was perfect, and then see yourself for who you are because you're an accomplished person.

A: I have to heal a younger part of myself because I've healed that part up until maybe about elementary school, because I have accomplished a lot but there's kind of that root base still that I haven't been able to get to yet, and over time it regresses back a little more, and I slowly am able to heal it. You repeat it spirally each time a deeper level.
F: It's fantastic that you're aware of that. Yes, by looking at your past, you can start healing that part of you. Let that part of you know you're doing fine. Talk to him. Say "I am Alex, and I am this age. I am doing fine". Start telling yourself so you can start healing that child within you, because that little child is wounded. That little child is very lonely; that little child is isolated and scared so you need to heal the little child within you because that's you. There's no

past or future, it's all in the present. It's carried with you until this day, so you're going to release that. Until you release it, you carry that burden on your shoulder, and all this pain that people gave you is lodged within you. Even though you may not know exactly where it is, that's part of what's been taken into your fiber.

A: Yeah, again the way I see it is almost like a magnet, people repeat patterns a lot for a reason.

F: Because of the programming.

A: Yeah again it's kind of took me stepping back this year, coming to realize "Oh wait this isn't normal", but again it's always tracing back to see where that pattern was programmed, and why is it being repeated.

F: You went through all those experiences, but once you deprogram yourself, you have taken so much off your load. You're going to be a completely different person. You're going to find your joy because right now to find your joy, you have to dig. Your joy will exude out of you.

A: I've had those radiant moments so I know what you're referring to.

F: You've got to get to that, you can live that way, once you are able to de-program yourself, which you can. Experience the freedom that comes out of detangling. From this moment on, make a promise that you're going to take care of yourself better. You're going to tell yourself to back off, you're fine, okay? Even if you make a mistake, you're going to tell yourself it's fine. Even if someone criticizes you, you're going to say it's fine because this is the virtual reality you're living in. It has its ups and downs and that's what it is. If you start finding yourself tensing up, take another deep breath. Your breath can help you. Your breath is what connects you to you. When you are seeing someone projecting something negative to you, let them know "I don't want to accept your projection of what you think I am, you can keep it to yourself".

<u>A:</u> Thank you. This was good.

Made in the USA
San Bernardino, CA
10 November 2018